THE WIDOW RANTER

THE WIDOW RANTER

Aphra Behn

a *Broadview Anthology of British Literature* edition

Contributing Editor, *The Widow Ranter*:
Adrienne L. Eastwood, San José State University

General Editors,
Broadview Anthology of British Literature:
Joseph Black, University of Massachusetts, Amherst
Leonard Conolly, Trent University
Kate Flint, University of Southern California
Isobel Grundy, University of Alberta
Wendy Anne Lee, New York University
Don LePan, Broadview Press
Roy Luizza, University of Tennessee
Jerome J. McGann, University of Virginia
Anne Lake Prescott, Barnard College
Jason Rudy, University of Maryland
Claire Waters, University of California, Davis

broadview press

BROADVIEW PRESS – www.broadviewpress.com
Peterborough, Ontario, Canada

Founded in 1985, Broadview Press remains a wholly independent publishing house. Broadview's focus is on academic publishing: our titles are accessible to university and college students as well as scholars and general readers. With over 800 titles in print, Broadview has become a leading international publisher in the humanities, with world-wide distribution. Broadview is committed to environmentally responsible publishing and fair business practices.

Library and Archives Canada Cataloguing in Publication

Title: The Widow Ranter / Aphra Behn ; contributing editor, The Widow Ranter:
    Adrienne L. Eastwood, San José State University.
Names: Behn, Aphra, 1640-1689, author. | Eastwood, Adrienne L., editor.
Series: Broadview anthology of British literature edition.
Description: Series statement: Broadview anthology of British literature edition | Includes
    bibliographical references.
Identifiers: Canadiana (print) 20220217637 | Canadiana (ebook) 20220217653 | ISBN
    9781554815739 (softcover) | ISBN 9781770488618 (PDF) | ISBN 9781460407974 (EPUB)
Subjects: LCSH: Behn, Aphra, 1640-1689—Criticism and interpretation. | LCSH: Bacon's
    Rebellion, 1676—Drama. | LCGFT: Drama.
Classification: LCC PR3317 .W54 2022 | DDC 822/.4—dc23

Broadview Press handles its own distribution in North America:
PO Box 1243, Peterborough, Ontario K9J 7H5, Canada
555 Riverwalk Parkway, Tonawanda, NY 14150, USA
Tel: (705) 743-8990; Fax: (705) 743-8353
email: customerservice@broadviewpress.com

For all territories outside of North America, distribution is handled by Eurospan Group.

Broadview Press acknowledges the financial support of the Government of Canada for our publishing activities.

Canada

Developmental Editor: Helena Snopek
Cover Designer: Lisa Brawn
Typesetter: George Kirkpatrick

Contents

Introduction

Aphra Behn
1640–1689

Long recognized as the first professional woman writer in England,
Aphra Behn was one of the most prolific dramatists of the Restoration period and has been credited with introducing into her plays,
to an unprecedented degree, aspects of the life of the time not previ-
ously considered fit material for the stage. But much as Behn was
successful and influential in her own day, by the late nineteenth
century she was almost forgotten; the open treatment of sexuality—
including interracial relationships—in her work was condemned as
too coarse to be deserving of a broad audience. In the twentieth century, however, her literary reputation soared anew, and she has since
been championed by feminists for creating a place for women in the
writing world. Virginia Woolf wrote in *A Room of One's Own*: "All
women together ought to let flowers fall upon the tomb of Aphra
Behn, … for it was she who earned them the right to speak their
minds."

Little is known about Behn's early life with any certainty, including her parentage. Some claim she was born to a barber and his wife,
the Amies, in Wye, Kent, but scholars now generally accept that she
was born to a family called Johnson just outside Canterbury. There
is some documentary evidence to suggest that she married a man
named John Halse in 1657. Not long thereafter the family appears to
have moved to Surinam in South America, where her father had been
given an administrative post, and to have remained there until about
1663, even after her father's death. Her stay in the then-British colony
would have exposed Behn to what would become the setting of her
most enduringly famous work, the prose narrative *Oroonoko* (1688),
more than twenty years later. Behn likely wrote her first play, *The
Young King*, shortly after her return to England (though it would not
be produced until 1679).

It is generally assumed that Behn acquired the surname by which she went throughout her adult life by marrying Johan Behn, a merchant of Dutch/German heritage—though no concrete evidence of their marriage has surfaced. He may have died in 1664, possibly of the bubonic plague, or the couple may have separated; at any rate, no record of him after this point has come down to us. Some time during the mid-1660s, Behn was introduced to the court of Charles II. She was considered a witty conversationalist, and her travels to the colonies made her much sought after. Her knowledge of several languages, including Dutch, proved useful and in 1666 she became a spy for the king in Antwerp. She was Agent 160, also known as Astrea, a name she used later as a *nom de plume*. She incurred a great deal of debt while working in the king's service, and when she returned to London in 1667 she may have spent a brief period in debtor's prison.

As a single woman with no other source of income, Behn became a writer out of necessity. She wrote in one of her prefaces that she was "forced to write for bread and not ashamed to own it." This was a period of new freedom for women; with the Restoration of the monarchy in 1660, following a decade of suppression under Puritan rule, the theaters had re-opened, and women were for the first time appearing on the commercial stage in England, as they already did in France. Behn was able to find a niche in a newly burgeoning theater world that was looking for new works to produce. Her first play to be produced on stage was *The Forced Marriage* (1670). Its central theme—the human damage caused when parents forced their children, particularly their daughters, to marry against their free choice—was present in many of her later plays as well. Behn would often use her plays to attack what she considered the wrongs of society.

The world of Restoration drama was one tolerant of iconoclasm, and in that context it is less surprising than it might otherwise be that Behn became one of the most established dramatists of the time, writing approximately twenty plays in as many years. The years 1676–83 comprised her most successful period of writing, and from this period *The Rover* (1677) remains the play she is most known for. Like many of her plays, *The Rover* was a social comedy, involving a good deal of sexual adventure (and misadventure). It was said to be one of the king's favorites and it was frequently produced through to the end of the century.

Between 1683 and 1689 Behn turned her attention to more experimental genres. Her last two texts are respectively among her best known and least known works: the non-dramatic narrative *Oroonoko* and the tragicomedy *The Widow Ranter*, both of which are set in the colonized Americas. While both works engage with issues associated with imperial power and revolt, only *Oroonoko* had a tangible influence on contemporary social discourses, becoming a literary touchstone for the antislavery movement. *The Widow Ranter* was produced for the stage five months after Behn's death, but after only one performance, it was proclaimed a terrific flop. Nevertheless, the two works and their respective treatments of colonization and depictions of Indigenous peoples offer an illuminating engagement with contemporary polemics surrounding British imperialism.

Behn's last few years were troubled by poverty and illness. She was aging, and no longer sought after for her witty repartee. She died on 16 April 1689; few of the details of her death are known. The epitaph on her tombstone in Westminster Abbey reads as follows: "Here lies a proof that wit can never be / Defence enough against mortality."

Historical background to *The Widow Ranter*: Bacon's Rebellion

The Widow Ranter is set in colonial Virginia during the conflict known as Bacon's Rebellion (1676–77), a violent revolt that saw hundreds of colonists rise up against the colonial government and embark on a mission to "ruin and extirpate all Indians in General," as declared in the *Manifesto* (1676) of the rebellion's leader, Nathaniel Bacon. But far from an isolated instance of settler discontent, Bacon's Rebellion had roots in the complex interplay of various wars and in the shifting of national and colonial boundaries that had been taking place in North America over the course of the seventeenth century, as European settlers sought political and economic dominance in the region. By the 1670s, myriad tenuous alliances and trade treaties existed among the various Indigenous peoples and colonial governments occupying the northeast and the Atlantic coast. These alliances, however, were not always supported by colonists. In Virginia, many farmers and traders felt that governor William Berkeley's tendency to favor diplomacy with Indigenous groups came at the expense of their own interests; these frustrations intensified in the wake of disputes such as that which arose in early 1675 between a group of Doeg traders and planters residing along the Potomac River. Believing themselves to have been cheated in a recent trade deal, the Doegs raided several English farms, stealing property and livestock. The affected colonists responded with a violent attack on what they believed to be a Doeg village, but inadvertently killed numerous of its Susquehannock residents—themselves having been driven into the region through ongoing warfare with the Haudenosaunee further north—as well. The mistake was disastrous, and swiftly destroyed Virginia's decades-long alliance with the Susquehannock, sending ripple effects through their relationships with other Indigenous peoples. Governor Berkeley's response—which included declaring war against the Susquehannock but mandated that civilians seek formal commissions before retaliating to Susquehannock attacks—was seen by many colonists as weak and ineffectual, and rumors of conspiracy between the colonial government and Indigenous groups began to spread.

Bacon, a relative newcomer to Virginia, sought to take advantage of these growing fears and frustrations, despite his lack of familiarity with the nuances of the colony's relationships with different Indigenous groups. Unable or unwilling to distinguish between those nations deemed by the colonial government to be friendly versus those declared hostile, Bacon helped to mobilize colonial antipathy toward all Indigenous nations indiscriminately—an antipathy made all the more easily manipulable by news of other wars between settlers and Indigenous peoples, such as King Philip's War (1675–78), coming out of other colonies around the same time.

The rebellion, which took place between 1676 and 1677, unfolded around what came to be a highly personal conflict between Berkeley and Bacon. The animosity between the two men caused Berkeley to remove Bacon from his seat on the Governor's Council, and on at least one occasion, Berkeley is reported to have stripped to the waist and dared Bacon to kill him. The acrimony hit a fever pitch in September of 1676 when Bacon's men tracked down Berkeley and his army hiding out on an estate near Old Plantation Creek. Berkeley, however, got the better of Bacon, captured his ships, and had several of Bacon's men hanged for sedition. Afterward, Berkeley easily took possession of Jamestown, but within a week, Bacon and his men forced Berkeley back into hiding, and when they realized that they did not have enough men to hold the town, they burned it to the ground, torching homes, taverns, and even the town's church. Berkeley could do nothing but watch it burn. Bacon then returned to the forests searching for other Indigenous people to destroy, but on 26 October 1676, he died suddenly from "bloody flux"—a mixture of typhus and dysentery. The rest of the rebel army were either "reduced to obedience" or executed.

The Widow Ranter

The Widow Ranter, which heavily fictionalizes these events, has received relatively little critical or popular attention compared to Behn's better-known comedies, such as *The Rover* (1677). Yet as one of few plays—if not the only play—by a British playwright to be set in colonial Virginia, and as the only one constructed around the historical rebellion led by Nathaniel Bacon, it is a fascinating addition to the existing body of transatlantic texts.

News of Bacon's Rebellion created a cultural stir in London, where pamphlets reporting the events began circulating in 1677. *Strange News from Virginia* (1677) and then *More News from Virginia* (1677) gave interested people information about Bacon's birth, education, and the events that led him to the colonies, as well as those that compelled him to wage war on the Indigenous population and to keep up these attacks in spite of repeated efforts by the colonial government to quell them. The pamphlets contributed to an ongoing discourse surrounding the cultural and political effects of colonization on England. While many people regarded the American colonies pridefully as part of the advancement of the British Empire, many also bemoaned the difficulties of maintaining control and governance across an ocean, and still more were conscious of the challenge of reconciling England's presence in Virginia with the pre-existing land claims of its Indigenous peoples.

Yet by the time that Behn was writing *The Widow Ranter*, over a decade after these events, the controversy surrounding Bacon's Rebellion was far from most people's minds, and so her choice to set her play amidst the turmoil of those events is an unusual one. In 1688, a period known as the Glorious Revolution, the overriding cultural concerns in England were about politics and religion as the overtly Catholic King James II was deposed and replaced with the Protestant duo King William and Queen Mary. In the midst of such tumultuous times, *The Widow Ranter* instead looks back to the very different and comparatively remote upheaval of Bacon's uprising in America. Perhaps Behn saw a connection between the political chaos of her own moment and the crisis of government at the crux of Bacon's Rebellion.

In Behn's retelling, Bacon is a noble and heroic figure who takes matters into his own hands when the inept colonial government fails to protect its people from hostile Indigenous groups. Rather than having an antipathy against all Indigenous people, the fictional Bacon is in a hopeless love triangle with the Indigenous King Cavarnio and his wife Queen Semernia, against whom he is ultimately forced into combat.

The tragic plotline featuring Bacon is balanced in the play by a comic one featuring the hard-drinking, tobacco-smoking Widow Ranter, who woos and wins Bacon's first lieutenant Daring by dressing as a soldier and pursuing him into the battlefield. The Widow's first husband had bought her "off the boat" as an indentured servant—a common arrangement for poor individuals seeking to emigrate to the colonies—married her, and then died, leaving her wealthy. Behn names this character after a radical sect of religious dissenters, the Ranters, who rejected traditional Christian doctrines, believing instead that sin is a construct. According to pamphlets written by the group's leading figures, the Ranters prided themselves on practices usually considered licentious or immoral, including copious drinking, smoking, and indiscriminate sexual activity, which likely extended to women as well as to men.

The history of the Ranters in England is itself tied to the politics of the English Civil War (1642–51), the defining conflict of Aphra Behn's life. During this period, the English fought over their form of government, with Royalists arguing that power should lie with the monarch, and Parliamentarians (also known as Roundheads) believing that the democratic parliament should have more clout. Behn, an outspoken Royalist as an adult, had grown up during this period, and came of age during the Interregnum (the period in which England did not have a monarch). When she was nine or ten, the Ranters became a popular target of political satirists who wished to link their professed lack of sexual restraint and rejection of sectarian conventions with the disorder and chaos associated with the fall of the English monarchy. Although some controversy exists surrounding the size and popularity of the sect, anti-Ranter sentiment was apparently widespread in England, particularly in the 1650s.

The question of why Behn chose to connect the titular heroine of her last play with an obscure religious group from thirty years prior to the play's historical setting is one of many that circulate around this work, making it particularly engaging material. Behn's decision to construct this play in a hybrid dramatic mode—the tragicomedy—signals a certain deliberate ambiguity that she sustains throughout the work. The cross-dressing of the female characters in both the comic and the tragic plotlines are ripe for queer and gender analyses, the depiction of the "Indian King and Queen"—who are simultaneously Europeanized and othered—has inspired postcolonial critique, and the uniqueness of a play set in colonial America with ties to both England and Virginia has sustained discourse about national identity and expansion. Questions about the tenuous nature of ruling rebellious subjects across an ocean are further engaged by Behn's play, in which she replaces the historical Governor William Berkeley (initially appointed in the 1640s by King Charles I, and reappointed in 1660 by Charles II) with a fictional Deputy Governor named Colonel Wellman. The play unfolds in a power vacuum: Berkeley is on his way from England with forces to assist the Virginians with Bacon's Rebellion, but he never arrives, and the governance of the colonies is left in the hands of a group of drunken clowns making legal decisions between bowls of rum punch.

Setting the play in Virginia similarly taps into polemic discourses about colonization that circulated in both Britain and America. People clearly had opinions about the "New World," some of whom would have seen in it the possibility for redemption—a chance to fashion a new identity or to pursue financial opportunities unavailable to them in England—while others might have viewed it as a venue for escape and indulgence. Through the two main characters, the play embraces both positions: Bacon is described as "a man indeed above the common rank," seeking his fortune from the land, while the Widow, of whom we know little except that she began her life in Virginia in servitude, may well have been a convict in England.

While many characters observe Bacon's "nobility," the Widow is more readily embraced for her generosity and admired for her ability to drink punch and smoke tobacco.

In spite of all of these fascinating layers—or perhaps because of them—*The Widow Ranter* was a flop. After only one production in 1689, the play went straight to print. This fact, too, is a seductive one. Were English audiences simply uninterested in a play set in Virginia? Did the interracial, adulterous love triangle go too far? In a prefatory letter to the 1690 print edition, the publisher blames the play's lack of success on the "ill nature of the critics," as well as on various questionable directorial decisions, but the text did not go into subsequent printings, so readership for the work wasn't robust either. Complicating matters further, Behn's *Oroonoko* enjoyed tremendous popularity, especially after it was adapted for the stage by Thomas Southerne in 1695.

Whatever the answers to these provocative questions, *The Widow Ranter* is an important work with much to add to the discourse on transatlantic literature, British imperialism, and colonization. Behn's treatment of the Indigenous characters both frankly addresses the "ungrateful theme" of usurpation while nevertheless reflecting her own culture's prejudices and perceptions of racialized difference. As one of the few early British works set in America, this one rewards readers with a sensational tale about a complicated period in global history.

A Note on the Text

This text is based on the 1690 edition held by the Huntingdon Library and accessed on the Early English Books Online database. Janet Todd's *Oroonoko, The Rover and Other Works* (Penguin, 1992) and Aaron R. Walden's *The Widow Ranter: or, The History of Bacon in Virginia* (Garland Publishing, 1993) have also been consulted. Spelling and punctuation have been modernized in accordance with the practices of *The Broadview Anthology of British Literature*.

The Widow Ranter;
or, The History of Bacon in Virginia
A Tragi-Comedy

DRAMATIS PERSONAE

Indian King, *called Cavarnio*
Bacon, *General of the English*
Colonel Wellman, *Deputy Governor*
Colonel Downright, *a loyal, honest colonel*

Hazard, Friendly, *two friends known to one another many years in England*
Daring, Fearless, *Lieutenant-Generals to Bacon*

Dullman, *a Captain*

Timorous Cornet, Whimsey, Whiff, Boozer, *Justices of the Peace, and very great cowards*

Brag, *a Capitan*
Grubb, *one complained on by Capitan Whiff for calling his wife a whore*
Mr. Blunt, *a petitioner against Brag*
Parson Dunce, *formerly a farrier,*[1] *fled from England, and Chaplain to the Governor*
Clerk
Boy [Jack]

Indian Queen, *called Semernia, beloved by Bacon*
Madam Surelove, *beloved by Hazard*
Mrs. Chrisante, *daughter to Colonel Downright*
Widow Ranter, *in love with Daring*

---

1   *farrier* One who shoes or cares for horses.

Mrs. Flirt
Mrs. Whimsey
Mrs. Whiff
Two Maids
[Nell]
Priests, Indians, Coachmen, Soldiers, with other Attendants

SCENE: Virginia, in Bacon's camp.

ACT I, SCENE I

(A room with several tables.)

(Enter Hazard in a travelling habit and a Sea-Boy carrying his port-mantle.[1])

HAZARD. What town's this, boy?

BOY. James-Town, master.

HAZARD. Take care my trunk be brought ashore tonight, and there's for your pains.

BOY. God bless you Master.   5

HAZARD. What do you call this house?

BOY. Mrs. Flirt's, Master, the best house for commendation in all Virginia.

HAZARD. That's well, has she any handsome ladies, sirrah?[2]

BOY. Oh! She's woundly[3] handsome herself Master, and the kindest   10
gentlewoman!

[Enter Mrs. Flirt and her maid Nell.]

God bless you, Mistress, I have brought you a young gentleman here.

FLIRT. That's well, honest Jack—sir, you are most heartily welcome.

HAZARD. Madam, your servant. *(Salutes her.)*   15

FLIRT. Please you to walk into a chamber, sir.

HAZARD. By and by madam, but I'll repose here a while for the coolness of the air.

FLIRT. This is a public room, sir, but 'tis at your service.

HAZARD. Madam, you oblige me.   20

FLIRT. A fine spoken person—a gentleman, I'll warrant him. Come Jack. I'll give thee a cogue[4] of brandy for old acquaintance.

---

1   *port-mantle*   Portmanteau; luggage bag.
2   *sirrah*   Term of address that conveys social inferiority.
3   *woundly*   Wonderfully.
4   *cogue*   Small wooden cup or drinking vessel.

(*Exeunt Landlady and Boy.*)

(*Hazard pulls out pen, ink, and paper, and goes to write. Enter Friendly.*)

FRIENDLY. Here Nell, a tankard of cool drink quickly.

NELL. You shall have it, sir.

25 FRIENDLY. Hah! Who's that stranger? He seems to be a gentleman.

HAZARD. (*Aside.*) If I should give credit to mine eyes, that should be Friendly.

FRIENDLY. Sir, you seem a stranger. May I take the liberty to present my service to you?

30 HAZARD. If I am not mistaken, sir, you are the only man in the world whom I would soonest pledge. You'll credit me if three years' absence has not made you forget Hazard.

FRIENDLY. Hazard, my friend! Come to my arms and heart!

HAZARD. This unexpected happiness o'er joys me. Who could have

35 imagined to have found thee in Virginia? I thought thou hadst been in Spain with thy brother.

FRIENDLY. I was so till ten months since when my uncle Colonel Friendly, dying here, left me a considerable plantation. And faith, I find diversions not altogether to be despised. The God

40 of Love reigns here with as much power as in courts or popular cities. But prithee, what chance (fortunate for me) drove thee to this part of the New World?

HAZARD. Why (faith), ill company and that common vice of the town, gaming, soon run out my younger brother's fortune,[1]

45 for imagining like some of the luckier gamesters to improve my stock at the Groom Porter's,[2] ventured on and lost all. My elder brother, an errant Jew,[3] had neither friendship nor honour enough to support me, but at last, was mollified by persuasions

---

1 *the town* I.e., London; *my younger brother's fortune* Primogeniture, the practice of passing down one's estate to the eldest male child, often left younger children financially dependent on their siblings. As a younger brother, Hazard squandered his inheritance on gambling, and then found that his older brother was reluctant to support him.

2 *Groom Porter* Royal official who oversaw matters of gaming and gambling, including deciding disputes.

3 *errant Jew* Antisemitic slur meaning a cheater at cards.

and the hopes of being forever rid of me, sent me hither with a small cargo to seek my fortune.   50

FRIENDLY. And begin the world withal.

HAZARD. I thought this a better venture than to turn sharping bully, cully in prentices and country squires, with my pocket full of false dice, your high and low flats and bars,[1] or turn broker to young heirs. Take up goods to pay tenfold at the death of their   55 fathers and take fees on both sides, or set up all night at the Groom Porter's begging his honour to go a guinea the better of the lay.[2] No, Friendly, I had rather starve abroad than live pitied and despised at home.

FRIENDLY. Thou art in the right, and art come just in the nick of   60 time to make thy fortune. Wilt thou follow my advice?

HAZARD. Thou art too honest to command anything that I shall refuse.

FRIENDLY. You must know then, there is about a mile from James-Town a young gentlewoman—no matter for her birth, her   65 breeding's the best this world affords—she is married to one of the richest merchants here. He is old and sick, and now gone into England for the recovery of his health where he'll e'en give up the ghost. He has writ her word he finds no amendment and resolves to stay another year. The letter I accidentally took up   70 and have about me. 'Tis easily counterfeited and will be of great use to us.

HAZARD. Now do I fancy I conceive thee.

FRIENDLY. Well, hear me first. You shall get another letter writ like this character[3] which shall say you are his kinsman that is come   75 to traffic in this country, and 'tis his will you should be received into his house as such.

HAZARD. Well, and what will come of this?

FRIENDLY. Why, thou art young and handsome, she young and desiring, 'twere easy to make her love thee, and if the old gentle-   80 man chance to die, you guess the rest—you are no fool.

---

1 *sharping* Swindling or cheating; *bully* Friend; *cully* Dupe or deceive; *pren-tices* Apprentices; i.e., young, inexperienced workers; *flats and bars* Different types of fake dice.
2 *to go ... the lay* I.e., to improve the odds.
3 *like this character* I.e., in the same handwriting; forged.

HAZARD. Aye, but if he should return—

FRIENDLY. If—why, if she love you, that other will be but a slender
bar to thy happiness. For if thou canst not marry her, thou
85   mayst lie with her, and gad, a younger brother may pick out a
pretty livelihood here that way, as well as in England. Or, if this
fail, there thou wilt find a perpetual visitor, the Widow Ranter,
a woman bought from the ship[1] by old Colonel Ranter. She
served him half a year, and then he married her, and dying in a
90   year more, left her worth fifty thousand pounds sterling, besides
plate and jewels. She's a great gallant,[2] but assuming the humour
of the country gentry, her extravagancy is very pleasant—she
retains something of her primitive quality still, but is good-
natured and generous.
95   HAZARD. I like all this well.

FRIENDLY. But I have a further end in this matter. You must know
there is in the same house a young heiress, one Colonel Downright's daughter, whom I love, I think not in vain. Her father
indeed has an implacable hatred for me, for which reason I can
100 but seldom visit her, and in this affair, I have need of a friend in
that house.

HAZARD. Me you're sure of.

FRIENDLY. And thus you'll have an opportunity to manage both our
amours. Here you will find occasion to show your courage as
105 well as express your love. For at this time the Indians, by our ill
management of trade, whom we have armed against ourselves,[3]
very frequently make war upon us with our own weapons,
though often coming by the worst, are forced to make peace
with us again. But so, as upon every turn they fall to massacring
110 us whenever we lie exposed to them.

HAZARD. I heard the news of this in England which hastens the new

---

1   *bought from the ship*   Reference to the practice of indentured servitude, in which a
migrant travels to the colonies and has their passage paid upon arrival by someone in need
of a servant. A contract is then negotiated, and once the agreed-upon term is served, the
migrant is released from their position. Such indentures were sometimes imposed upon
persons convicted of crimes, in a practice known as transportation.
2   *gallant*   Generally this designates a fashionable or well-dressed person, but it is a term
more commonly used to describe gentlemen rather than ladies; it also carries the connotation of being amorous.
3   *whom we ... against ourselves*   I.e., whom we have provided with weapons through trade.

governor's arrival here who brings you fresh supplies.

FRIENDLY. Would he were landed. We hear he is a noble gentleman.

HAZARD. He has all the qualities of a gallant man—besides, he is
nobly born. 115

FRIENDLY. This country wants nothing but to be peopled with a
well-born race to make it one of the best colonies in the world.
But for want of a governor we are ruled by a council, some of
which have been perhaps transported criminals,[1] who having
acquired great estates, are now become Your Honour, and Right 120
Worshipful, and possess all places of authority. There are among
them some honest gentlemen who now begin to take upon them
and manage affairs as they ought to be.

HAZARD. Bacon, I think, was one of the council.

FRIENDLY. Now you have named a man indeed above the common 125
rank—by nature generous, brave, resolved, and daring—who,
studying the lives of the Romans[2] and great men that have raised
themselves to the most elevated fortunes, fancies it easy for
ambitious men to aim at any pitch of glory. I've heard him often
say, "Why cannot I conquer the universe as well as Alexander?[3] 130
Or like another Romulus[4] form a new Rome and make myself
adored?"

HAZARD. Why might he not? Great souls are born in common men,
sometimes, as well as princes.

FRIENDLY. This thirst of glory cherished by sullen melancholy, I 135
believe, was the first motive that made him in love with the
young Indian queen, fancying no hero ought to be without his
princess. And this was the reason why he so earnestly pressed
for a commission to be made general against the Indians, which
long was promised him. But they, fearing his ambition, still put 140
him off till the grievances grew so high that the whole country
flocked to him and begged he would redress them. He took
the opportunity and led them forth to fight, and vanquishing

---

1   *transported criminals*   I.e., convicts sentenced to be exiled to the colonies.
2   *the lives of the Romans*   Probable allusion to Greek writer Plutarch's *Parallel Lives* (c. second
    century BCE), a famous series of biographies of great men from Greek and Roman history.
3   *Alexander*   Macedonian conqueror Alexander the Great (356–323 BCE), who formed one
    of the largest empires in history.
4   *Romulus*   Legendary founder of Rome.

brought the enemy to fair terms, but now instead of receiving
145   him as a conqueror, we treat him as a traitor.
HAZARD. Then it seems all the crime this brave fellow has committed is serving his country without authority.
FRIENDLY. 'Tis so, and however I admire the man, I am resolved to be of the contrary party that I may make an interest in our new
150   governor. Thus stands affairs so that after you have seen Madam Surelove, I'll present you to the council for a commission.
HAZARD. But my kinsman's character—
FRIENDLY. He was a Leicestershire younger brother, came over hither with a small fortune, which his industry has increased to
155   a thousand pound a year, and he is now Colonel John Surelove, and one of the council.
HAZARD. Enough.
FRIENDLY. About it then. Madam Flirt to direct you.
HAZARD. You are full of your Madams here.
160 FRIENDLY. Oh! 'Tis the greatest affront imaginable to call a woman "Mistress,"[1] though but a retail brandy-monger. Adieu! One thing more: tomorrow is our country court, pray do not fail to be there for the rarity of the entertainment. But I shall see you anon at Surelove's where I'll salute thee as my first meeting and
165   as an old acquaintance in England.—Here's company. Farewell.
(*Exit Friendly.*)

(*Enter Dullman, Timorous, and Boozer. Hazard sits at a table and writes.*)

DULLMAN. Here Nell—Well Lieutenant Boozer, what are you for?

(*Enter Nell.*)

BOOZER. I am for cooling Nants,[2] Major.
DULLMAN. Here Nell, a quart of Nants and some pipes and smoke.

---

1 *your Madams ... "Mistress"* In England, "Madam" as a term of address was generally reserved for persons of higher status than the speaker, such as for servants addressing employers. Hazard draws attention to the fact that in Jamestown, English conventions are not replicated.
2 *Nants* Type of brandy.

TIMOROUS. And do ye hear Nell, bid your mistress come in to joke   170
a little with us, for gadzoors,[1] I was damnable drunk last night
and am better at the petticoat than the bottle today.

DULLMAN. Drunk last night and sick today! How comes that about,
Mr. Justice? You used to bear your brandy well enough.

TIMOROUS. Aye, your shier-brandy I'll grant ye, but I was drunk at   175
Colonel Downright's with your high Burgundy claret.[2]

DULLMAN. A pox on that paulter[3] liquor—your English French
wine. I wonder how the gentlemen drink it.

TIMOROUS. Aye, so do I. 'Tis for want of a little Virginia breeding.
How much more like a gentleman 'tis to drink as we do, brave,   180
edifying punch[4] and brandy. But they say, the young noblemen
now and sparks in England begin to reform and take it for their
morning's draught, get drunk by noon, and despise the lousy
juice of the grape.

(*Enter Mrs. Flirt.*)

DULLMAN. Come landlady, come. You are so taken up with Parson   185
Dunce that your old friends can't drink a dram with you. What?
No smutty catch now, no gibe or joke to make the punch go
down merrily and advance trading? Nay, they say, gad forgive ye,
you never miss going to church when Mr. Dunce preaches. But
here's to you. (*Drinks.*)   190

FLIRT. Lords, your Honours are pleased to be merry—but my
service to your Honour. (*Drinks.*)

HAZARD. (*Aside.*) Honours, who the devil have we here? Some of
the wise council at least. I'd sooner take them for hogherds.

FLIRT. Say what you please of the doctor, but I'll swear he's a fine   195
gentleman. He makes the prettiest sonnets, nay, and sings them
himself to the rarest tunes.

TIMOROUS. Nay, the man will serve for both soul and body, for they

---

1   *gadzoors*   Slangy swear-word used in various forms by Timorous throughout the play.
2   *shier-brandy*   Locally produced brandy, with a suggestion of being "sheer" or less
    potent;   *high Burgundy claret*   Wine from the region of Burgundy in France.
3   *paulter*   Paltry; inferior.
4   *punch*   Here and throughout, a strong, alcoholic concoction.

200   say he was a farrier in England, but breaking,[1] turned life-guard
man,[2] and his horse dying—he counterfeited a deputation from
the bishop and came over here a substantial orthodox.[3] But
come, where stands the cup? Here, my service to you Major.

FLIRT. Your Honours are pleased—but methinks Doctor Dunce is a
very edifying person, and a gentleman (and I pretend[4] to know
205   a gentleman!), for I myself am a gentlewoman. My father was
a baronet, but undone in the late rebellion[5]—and I am fain to
keep an ordinary[6] now, heaven help me!

TIMOROUS. Good lack,[7] why see how virtue may be belied. We
heard your father was a tailor, but trusting for old Oliver's
210   funeral, broke and so came hither to hide his head![8] But my
service to you; what you are never the worse?

FLIRT. Your Honour knows this is a scandalous place, for they say
your Honour was but a broken excise man[9] who spent the king's
money to buy your wife fine petticoats, and at last, not worth a
215   groat,[10] you came over a poor servant, though now a Justice of
the Peace and of the Honourable Council.

TIMOROUS. Adzoors! If I knew who 'twas said so, I'd sue him for
Scandalum Magnatum.[11]

DULLMAN. Hang 'em, scoundrels, hang 'em! They live upon scandal,
220   and we are scandal proof! They say, too, that I was a tinker and
running the country, robbed a gentleman's house there, was

---

1 *breaking* Going broke

2 *life-guard man* Part of the cavalry of the British army.

3 *substantial orthodox* Upstanding person of good repute.

4 *pretend* Make claim to (not necessarily with an implication of falseness).

5 *baronet* Category of the gentry established by James I in 1611; a baronetcy is the lowest
hereditary honor; *late rebellion* Mrs. Flirt is referring to the English Civil War
(1642–49), which pitted the Parliamentarians, led by the Puritan Oliver Cromwell, against
the Royalists, and resulted in the beheading of Charles I. Cromwell served as Lord Protec-
tor of the Commonwealth of England, Scotland, and Ireland from 1653 to 1658.

6 *fain ... ordinary* Grateful to be able to run a pub.

7 *Good lack* Expression comparable to "my goodness."

8 *We heard ... his head!* Timorous suggests that Flirt's father lost his fortune working for
Oliver Cromwell, and that when the monarchy was restored in 1660, he came to Virginia
to avoid being held accountable for his association with the Commonwealth.

9 *Your Honour ... excise man* Flirt hints at a rumor that Timorous used his position in
England as a customs agent to commit fraud.

10 *groat* Silver coin worth four pence.

11 *Scandalum Magnatum* Latin: The slander of magnates.

put into Newgate,[1] got a reprieve after condemnation, and was transported hither. And that you, Boozer, were a common pickpocket, and being often flogged at the cart's-tale afterwards turned evidence,[2] and when the times grew honest was fain to fly. 225

BOOZER. Aye, aye, Major. If scandal would have broke our hearts, we had not arrived to the honour of being Privy Counsellors. But come, Mrs. Flirt, what, never a song to entertain us?

FLIRT. Yes, and a singer too, newly come ashore.

TIMOROUS. Adzoors, let's have it then. 230

(Enter girl, who sings; they bear the bob.)[3]

HAZARD. Here Maid, a tankard of your drink.

FLIRT. Quickly Nell. Wait upon the gentleman.

DULLMAN. Please you, sir, to taste our liquor? My service to you. I see you are a stranger and alone. Please you to come to our table? 235

(He rises and comes.)

FLIRT. Come sir, pray sit down here. These are very honourable persons, I assure you. This is Major Dullman, Major of his Justice of the Peace in Corum.[4] This is Captain Boozer, all of the Honourable Council.

HAZARD. With your leave, gentlemen. 240

(Sits.)

TIMOROUS. My service to you, sir.

(Drinks.)

What have you brought over any cargo, sir? I'll be your customer.

---

1   *tinker* Itinerant peddler;   *Newgate* London's main prison.
2   *Boozer ... turned evidence* Dullman suggests that Boozer was often punished as a thief, and that he was known to authorities as an informer.
3   *bear the bob* Join by singing the refrain.
4   *in Corum* Latin: for the Crown.

BOOZER. (*Aside.*) Aye and cheat him too, I'll warrant him.

245 HAZARD. I was not bred to merchandizing, sir, nor do intend to follow the drudgery of trading.

DULLMAN. Men of fortune seldom travel hither, sir, to see fashions.

TIMOROUS. Why, brother, it may be the gentleman has a mind to be a planter. Will you hire yourself to make a crop of tobacco this 250 year?

HAZARD. I was not born to work, sir.

TIMOROUS. Not work, sir, 'zoors, your betters have worked sir. I have worked myself, sir, both set and stripped tobacco, for all I am of the Honourable Council. Not work, quoth he. I suppose, 255 sir, you wear your fortune upon your back, sir?

HAZARD. Is it your custom here, sir, to affront strangers? I shall expect satisfaction!

(*Rises.*)

TIMOROUS. Why, does anybody here owe you anything?

DULLMAN. No, unless he means to be paid for drinking with us, ha 260 ha ha!

HAZARD. No sir, I have money to pay for what I drink. Here is my club[1]—my guinea.

(*Flings down a guinea.*)

I scorn to be obliged to such scoundrels!

BOOZER. Hum—call men of honour scoundrels. (*Rises in [a] huff.*)

265 TIMOROUS. Let him alone, let him alone, brother. How should he learn manners? He never was in Virginia before.

DULLMAN. He is some Covent-Garden[2] bully.

TIMOROUS. Or some broken citizen turned factor.[3]

HAZARD. Sir, you lie and you're a rascal.

(*Flings the brandy in [Timorous]'s face.*)

---

1 *club* Contribution to a shared bill.
2 *Covent-Garden* London's West End district noted at the time for its taverns, theaters, and brothels.
3 *broken ... factor* Bankrupt person who had become a mercantile agent.

TIMOROUS. Adzoors, he has spilled all the brandy!

(*Timorous runs behind the door, Dullman and Boozer strike Hazard.*)

HAZARD. I understand no cudgel-play but wear a sword to right myself.

(*Draws, they run off.*)

FLIRT. Good heavens, what quarrelling in my house?
HAZARD. Do the persons of quality in this country treat strangers thus?
FLIRT. Alas sir, 'tis a familiar way they have, sir.
HAZARD. I'm glad I know it. Pray, madam, can you inform one how I may be furnished with a horse and a guide to Madam Surelove's?
FLIRT. A most accomplished lady and my very good friend. You shall be immediately—

(*Exeunt.*)

ACT I, SCENE 2

[*The council table.*]

(*Enter Wellman, Downright, Dunce, Whimsey, Whiff, and others.*)

WELLMAN. Come Mr. Dunce, though you are no counsellor, yet your counsel may be good in times of necessity, as now.
DUNCE. If I may give worthy advice, I do not look upon our danger to be so great from the Indians as from young Bacon, whom the people have nicknamed "Fright-all."
WHIMSEY. Aye, aye, that same Bacon. I would he were well hanged! I am afraid that under pretense of killing all the Indians he means to murder us, lie with our wives, hang up our little children, and make himself lord and king.
WHIFF. Brother Whimsey, not so hot. With leave of the Honourable

Board, my wife is of the opinion that Bacon came seasonably to
our aid, and what he has done was for our defense. The Indians
came down upon us and ravished us all, men, women, and
children.

15 WELLMAN. If these grievances were not redressed we had our reasons
for it. It was not that we were insensible, Captain Whiff, of
what we suffered from the insolence of the Indians. But all knew
what we must expect from Bacon if that by lawful authority he
had arrived to so great a command as general, nor would we be
20 huffed[1] out of our commissions.

DOWNRIGHT. 'Tis most certain that Bacon did not demand a commission out of a design of serving us, but to satisfy his ambition
and his love—it being no secret that he passionately admires
the Indian Queen—and under the pretext of a war, intends to
25 kill the king her husband, establish himself in her heart, and on
all occasions, make himself a more formidable enemy than the
Indians are.

WHIMSEY. Nay, nay, I ever foresaw he would prove a villain.

WHIFF. Nay, and he be thereabout, my Nancy shall have no more to
30 do with him.

WELLMAN. But gentlemen, the people daily flock to him, so that his
army is too considerable for us to oppose by anything but policy.

DOWNRIGHT. We are sensible, gentlemen, that our fortunes, our
honours, and our lives are at stake, and therefore you are called
35 together to consult what is to be done in this grand affair till our
governor and forces arrive from England. The truce he made
with the Indians will be out tomorrow.

WHIFF. Ay, and then he intends to have another bout with the Indians. Let's have patience I say till he has thrummed their jackets,[2]
40 and then to work with your politics as soon as you please.

DOWNRIGHT. Colonel Wellman has answered that point, good
Captain Whiff, 'tis the event of this battle we ought to dread,
and if won or lost will be equally fatal for us, either from the
Indians or from Bacon.

---

1   *huffed* Scolded or chided.
2   *thrummed their jackets* Shredded their garments; used here as a euphemism for trouncing
    the enemy.

DUNCE. With the permission of the Honourable Board I think   45
I have hit upon an expedient that may prevent this battle.
Your Honours shall write a letter to Bacon where you shall
acknowledge his services, invite him kindly home, and offer him
a commission for general—

WHIFF. Just my Nancy's counsel. Doctor Dunce has spoken like   50
a cherub. He shall have my voice for general. What say you,
brother Whimsey?

DUNCE. I say he is a noble fellow and fit for a general. But conceive
me right, gentlemen, as soon as he shall have rendered himself,
seize him and strike off his head at the fort.   55

WHIFF. Hum! His head—brother.

WHIMSEY. Ay, ay, Doctor Dunce speaks like a cherub.

WELLMAN. Mr. Dunce, your counsel in extremity I confess is not
amiss, but I should be loth to deal dishonourably with any man.

DOWNRIGHT. His crimes deserve death. His life is forfeited by   60
law but shall never be taken by my consent by treachery. If by
any stratagem we could take him alive and either send him for
England to receive there his punishment or keep him prisoner
here till the governor arrive I should agree to it, but I question
his coming in upon our invitation.   65

DUNCE. Leave that to me—

WHIMSEY. Come, I'll warrant him, the rogue's as stout as Hector.[1]
He fears neither heaven nor hell.

DOWNRIGHT. He is too brave and bold to refuse our summons and
I am for sending him for England and leaving him to the King's   70
mercy.

DUNCE. In that you'll find more difficulty, sir. To take him off here
will be more quick and sudden, for the people worship him.

WELLMAN. I'll never yield to so ungenerous an expedient. The
seizing him I am content in the extremity wherein we are to   75
follow. What say you, Colonel Downright? Shall we send him a
letter now while this two days' truce lasts between him and the
Indians?

DOWNRIGHT. I approve it.

ALL. And I, and I, and I.   80

---

1 *stout* Strong and able; *Hector* Hero of Troy in the Trojan War.

DUNCE. If your Honours please to make me the messenger, I'll use some arguments of my own to prevail with him.

WELLMAN. You say well, Mr. Dunce, and we'll dispatch you presently.

(*Exeunt Wellman, Downright, and all but Whimsey, Whiff, and Dunce.*)

85 WHIFF. Ah, Doctor, if you could but have persuaded Colonel Wellman and Colonel Downright to have hanged him—

WHIMSEY. Why, brother Whiff, you were for making him a general but now.

WHIFF. The counsels of wise statesmen, brother Whimsey, must
90 change as causes do, d' ye see?

DUNCE. Your Honours are in the right, and whatever those two leading counsellors say, they would be glad if Bacon were dispatched—but the punctilio[1] of honour is such a thing.

WHIMSEY. Honour? A pox on't! What is that honour that keeps such
95 a bustle in the world yet never did good as I heard of?

DUNCE. Why, 'tis a foolish word only, taken up by great men, but rarely practiced. But if you would be great men indeed—

WHIFF. If we would, Doctor, name, name the way.

DUNCE. Why, you command each of you a company—when Bacon
100 comes from the camp, as I am sure he will (and, full of this silly thing called honour, will come unguarded too), lay some of your men in ambush along those ditches by the savannah about a mile from the town, and as he comes by, seize him and hang him upon the next tree.

105 WHIFF. Hum. Hang him! A rare plot.

WHIMSEY. (*Aside.*) Hang him! We'll do it! We'll do it sir, and I doubt not but to be made general for the action. I'll take it all upon myself.

DUNCE. If you resolve upon this, you must about it instantly. Thus
110 I shall at once serve my country and revenge myself on the rascal for affronting my dignity once at the council-table by calling me a farrier. (*Exit Doctor.*)[2]

---

1   *punctilio* Small or insignificant detail.
2   *Doctor* I.e., Dunce.

WHIFF. Do you know, brother, what we are to do?

WHIMSEY. To do? Yes. To hang a general, brother, that's all.

WHIFF. All, but is it lawful to hang any general? 115

WHIMSEY. Lawful? Yes. 'Tis lawful to hang any general that fights against law.

WHIFF. But in what he has done? He has served the king and our country, and preserved all our lives and fortunes.

WHIMSEY. That's all one, brother, if there be but a quirk in the 120 law offended in this case, though he fought like Alexander and preserved the whole world from perdition, yet if he did it against law, 'tis lawful to hang him. Why, what brother, is it fit that every impudent fellow that pretends to a little honour, loyalty, and courage, should serve his king and country against the law? 125 No, no, brother. These things are not to be suffered in a civil government by law established. Wherefore, let's about it.

(*Exeunt.*)

ACT I, SCENE 3

(*Surelove's house.*)

(*Enter Ranter and her coachman.*)

RANTER. Here Jeffery, ye drunken dog, set your coach and horses up. I'll not go till the cool of the evening. I love to ride in fresco.[1] (*Enter a boy.*)

COACHMAN. (*Aside.*) Yes, after hard drinking. [*Aloud.*] It shall be done, madam. 5

RANTER. How now, boy. Is Madam Surelove at home?

BOY. Yes, madam.

RANTER. Go tell her I am here, sirrah.

BOY. Who are you pray, forsooth?

RANTER. Why, you son of a baboon! Don't you know me? 10

BOY. No, madam. I came over but in the last ship.

---

1   *in fresco*   In the fresh air.

RANTER. What, from Newgate or Bridewell?[1] From shoving the
tumbler, sirrah, lifting or filing the cly?[2]

BOY. I don't understand this country's language yet, forsooth.

15 RANTER. You rogue. 'Tis what we transported from England first!
Go, ye dog, go tell your lady the Widow Ranter is come to dine
with her—(*Exit Boy.*) I hope I shall not find that rogue Daring
here, sniveling after Mrs. Chrisante. If I do, by the Lord, I'll lay
him thick. Pox on him! Why should I love the dog, unless it be a

20 judgement upon me.

(*Enter Surelove and Chrisante.*)

My dear jewel, how dost do? As for you, gentlewoman, you
are my rival, and I am in rancour against you till you have
renounced my Daring.

CHRISANTE. All the interest I have in him, madam, I resign to you.

25 RANTER. Aye—but your house lying so near the camp gives me
mortal fears. But prithee, how thrives thy amour with honest
Friendly?

CHRISANTE. As well as an amour can that is absolutely forbid by
a father on one side and pursued by a good resolution on the

30 other.

RANTER. Hay, gad, I'll warrant for Friendly's resolution, what,
though his fortune be not answerable to yours. We are bound to
help one another. Here, boy! Some pipes and a bowl of punch!
You know my humour, madam, I must smoke and drink in a

35 morning or I am mawkish[3] all day.

SURELOVE. But will you drink punch in a morning?

RANTER. Punch! 'Tis my morning draught, my table-drink, my
treat, my regalia, my everything! Ah my dear Surelove, if thou
wouldst but refresh and cheer thy heart with punch in a morn-

40 ing, thou wouldst not look thus cloudy all the day.

---

1 *Bridewell* Another of London's prisons, many of whose inmates were women convicted
of vagrancy or illicit sexual activity.

2 *shoving the tumbler* Slang: being punished by whipping; *lifting ... cly* Thieves' slang
for petty theft.

3 *mawkish* Sickly or weak.

(*Enter pipes and a great bowl; she falls to smoking.*)

SURELOVE. I have reason, madam, to be melancholy. I have received
a letter from my husband who gives me an account that he is
worse in England than when he was here, so that I fear I shall
see him no more. The doctors can do no good on him.
RANTER. A very good hearing. I wonder what the devil thou hast   45
done with him so long? An old fusty weather-beaten skeleton.
As here's to the next, may he be young, heaven, I beseech thee.
(*Drinks.*)
SURELOVE. You have reason to praise an old man who died and left
you worth fifty thousand pounds!   50
RANTER. Aye gad. And what's better, sweetheart, died in good time
too and left me young enough to spend this fifty thousand
pound in better company. Rest his soul for that too.
CHRISANTE. I doubt[1] 'twill be all laid out in Bacon's mad Lieutenant
General Daring.   55
RANTER. Faith I think I could lend it the rogue on good security.
CHRISANTE. What's that, to be bound body for body?
RANTER. Rather that he should love nobody's body besides my own.
But my fortune is too good to trust the rogue; my money makes
me an infidel.   60
CHRISANTE. You think they all love you for that.
RANTER. For that—Ay, what else? If it were not for that, I might sit
still and sigh, and cry out, "A miracle! A miracle!" at sight of a
man within my doors.

(*Enter Maid.*)

MAID. Madam, here's a young gentleman without[2] would speak   65
with you.
SURELOVE. With me? Sure thou'rt mistaken. Is it not Friendly?
MAID. No madam, 'tis a stranger.
RANTER. 'Tis not Daring, that rogue, is it?
MAID. No madam.   70

---

1 *doubt* Suspect; fear.
2 *without* Outside.

RANTER. Is he handsome? Does he look like a gentleman?

MAID. He is handsome and looks like a gentleman.

RANTER. Bring him in then. I hate a conversation without a fellow.

(*Enter Hazard with a letter.*)

    [*Aside.*] Hah! A good, handsome lad indeed!

75 SURELOVE. With me, sir, would you speak?

HAZARD. If you are Madam Surelove.

SURELOVE. So I am called.

HAZARD. Madam, I am newly arrived from England, and from your
    husband my kinsman I brought you this. (*Gives a letter.*)

80 RANTER. Please you to sit, sir.

HAZARD. (*Aside. Sits down.*) She's extremely handsome.

RANTER. Come sir, will you smoke a pipe?

HAZARD. I never do, madam.

RANTER. Oh, fie upon it! You must learn, then. We all smoke here,

85   'tis part of good breeding. Well, well, what cargo, what goods
    have ye? Any points, lace, rich stuffs,[1] jewels? If you have, I'll be
    your chafferer.[2] I live hard by. Anybody will direct you to the
    Widow Ranter's.

HAZARD. I have already heard of you, madam.

90 RANTER. What, you are like all the young fellows. The first thing
    they do when they come to a strange place is to inquire what
    fortunes there are.

HAZARD. Madam, I had no such ambition.

RANTER. Gad, then you're a fool, sir. But come, my service to you.

95   We rich widows are the best commodity this country affords, I'll
    tell you that.

(*This while [Surelove] reads the letter.*)

SURELOVE. Sir, my husband has recommended you here in a most
    particular manner, by which I do not only find the esteem he
    has for you, but the desire he has of gaining you mine, which

---

1 *points* Variety of needlework; *stuffs* Fabrics.

2 *chafferer* Dealer.

on a double score I render you first for his sake, next for those   100
merits that appear in yourself.

HAZARD. Madam, the endeavours of my life shall be to express my
gratitude for this great bounty.

(*Enter Maid.*)

MAID. Madam, Mr. Friendly's here.
SURELOVE. Bring him in.   105
HAZARD. Friendly—I had a dear friend of that name who I hear is
in these parts—pray heaven it may be he.

(*Enter Friendly.*)

RANTER. How now, Charles?[1]
FRIENDLY. Madam, your servant. Hah! Should not I know you for
my dear friend Hazard! (*Embracing him.*)   110
HAZARD. Or you're to blame my Friendly.
FRIENDLY. Prithee what calm brought thee ashore?
HAZARD. *Fortune de la guerre,*[2] but prithee ask me no questions in
so good company where a minute lost from this conversation is
a misfortune not to be retrieved.   115
FRIENDLY. (*Softly aside.*) Dost like her, rogue?
HAZARD. Like her? Have I sight or sense? Why, I adore her.
FRIENDLY. [*Aloud.*] My Chrisante, I heard your father would not be
here today, which made me snatch this opportunity of seeing
you.   120
RANTER. Come, come. A pox on this whining love; it spoils good
company!
FRIENDLY. You know, my dear friend, these opportunities come but
seldom, and therefore I must make use of them.
RANTER. Come, come. I'll give you a better opportunity at my   125
house tomorrow. We are to eat a buffalo there and I'll secure the
old gentleman from coming.
FRIENDLY. Then I shall see Chrisante once more before I go.

---

1 *Charles* Apparently Friendly's given name.
2 *Fortune de la guerre* French: the fortune of war.

CHRISANTE. Go? Heavens! Whither, my Friendly?

130 FRIENDLY. I have received a commission to go against the Indians, Bacon being sent for home.

RANTER. But will he come, being sent for?

FRIENDLY. If he refuse we are to endeavour to force him.

CHRISANTE. I do not think he will be forced, not even by Friendly.

135 FRIENDLY. And, faith, it goes against my conscience to lift my sword against him, for he is truly brave, and what he has done, a service to the country, had it but been by authority.

CHRISANTE. What pity 'tis there should be such false maxims in the world that noble actions, however great, must be criminal for
140 want of a law to authorize them.

FRIENDLY. Indeed, 'tis pity that when laws are faulty they should not be mended or abolished.

RANTER. Hark ye, Charles, by heaven, if you kill my Daring, I'll pistol you.

145 FRIENDLY. No, Widow. I'll spare him for your sake.

(*They join with Surelove.*)

HAZARD. Oh, she is all divine, and all the breath she utters serves but to blow my flame.

(*Enter Maid.*)

MAID. Madam, dinner is on the table.

SURELOVE. Please you, sir, to walk in? Come, Mr. Friendly.

(*She takes Hazard.*)

150 RANTER. Prithee, good wench, bring in the punch-bowl.

(*Exeunt.*)

ACT 2, SCENE I

(*A pavilion. Discovers*[1] *the Indian King and Queen*[2] *sitting in state with guards of Indians, men and women, attending to them; Bacon, richly dressed, attended by Daring, Fearless, and other Officers; he bows to the King and Queen who rise to receive him.*)

KING. I am sorry, sir, that we meet upon these terms—we who have so often embraced as friends.

BACON. (*Aside.*) How charming is the Queen! [*Aloud.*] War, sir, is not my business nor my pleasure. Nor was I bred in arms.[3] My country's good has forced me to assume a soldier's life. And 'tis   5
with much regret that I employ the first effects of it against my friends. Yet whilst I may—whilst this cessation lasts, I beg we may exchange those friendships, sir, we have so often paid in happier peace.

KING. For your part, sir, you've been so noble that I repent the   10
fatal difference that makes us meet in arms. Yet though I'm young, I'm sensible of injuries, and oft have heard my grandsire say that we were monarchs once of all this spacious world, till you—an unknown people landing here—distressed and ruined by destructive storms, abusing all of our charitable hospitality,   15
usurped our right and made your friends your slaves.

BACON. I will not justify the ingratitude of my forefathers, but finding here my inheritance, I am resolved still to maintain it so; and by my sword which first cut out my portion, defend each inch of land with my last drop of blood.   20

QUEEN. (*Aside.*) Even his threats have charms that please the heart.

KING. Come sir, let this ungrateful theme alone which is better disputed in the field.

---

1 *Discovers* Reveals.

2 *King and Queen* European terms that do not necessarily accurately reflect the forms of governance present in Indigenous societies. The character of Queen Semernia in this play is very loosely based on the historical Cockacoeske (c. 1640–86), who served as *warowan- skwa* of the Algonquian-speaking Pamunkey during the period of Bacon's Rebellion; she was referred to by the English as "Queen of the Pamunkey." Cockacoeske was among the signatories referred to as "Indian Kings and Queens" in the 1677 Treaty of Middle Plantation. See also the In Context materials at the end of this edition.

3 *bred in arms* Raised to be a soldier.

QUEEN. Is it impossible there might be wrought an understanding
25   betwixt my lord and you? 'Twas to that end I first desired this
        truce, myself proposing to be mediator, to which my Lord
        Cavarnio shall agree, could you but condescend. I know you're
        noble, and I have heard you say our tender sex could never plead
        in vain.
30 BACON. Alas! I dare not trust your pleading, madam. A few soft
        words from such a charming mouth would make me lay the
        conqueror at your feet as a sacrifice for all the ills he has done
        you.
   QUEEN. (*Aside.*) How strangely am I pleased to hear him talk.[1]
35 KING. Semernia, see—the dancers do appear. (*To Bacon.*) Sir, will
        you take your seat?

   (*He leads the Queen to a seat; they sit and talk.*)

   BACON. [*Aside.*] Curse on his sports that interrupted me! My
        very soul was hovering at my lip, ready to have discovered all
        its secrets. But oh! I dread to tell her of my pain, and when I
40   would, an awful trembling seizes me and she can only from
        my dying eyes read all the sentiments of my captive heart. (*Sits
        down; the rest wait.*)

   (*Enter Indians that dance antics;[2] after the dance, the King seems in
   discourse with Bacon, the Queen rises, and comes forth.*)

   QUEEN. The more I gaze upon this English stranger, the more
        confusion struggles in my soul. Oft I have heard of love, and oft
45   this gallant man (when peace had made him pay his idle visits)
        has told a thousand tales of dying aids. And ever when he spoke,
        my panting heart, with a prophetic fear, in sighs replied, I shall
        fall such a victim to his eyes.

---

1   This line and some intermittent subsequent lines appear to be in blank verse. It is possible
    that Behn, who did not live to see this work in either print or performance, may have
    intended to use poetry in a more sustained way throughout.
2   *dance antics* Behn uses a phrase that suggests that the movements of the dancers are
    "antic" or bizarre, reflecting her bias as a European commenting on a foreign culture.

(*Enter an Indian.*)

INDIAN. (*To the King.*) Sir, here's a messenger from the English
council desires admittance to the General.   50
BACON. (*To the King.*) With your permission, sir, he may advance.

(*Re-enter Indian with Dunce [holding] a letter.*)

DUNCE. All health and happiness attend your Honour. This is from
the Honourable Council. (*Gives him [the] letter.*)
KING. I'll leave you till you have dispatched the messenger, and then
expect your presence in the royal tent.   55

(*Exeunt King, Queen, and Indians.*)

BACON. (*To Daring.*) Lieutenant, read the letter.
DARING. (*Reads.*) "Sir, the necessity of what you have acted makes
it pardonable, and we could wish we had done the country and
ourselves so much justice as to have given you that commission
you desired. We now find it reasonable to raise more forces, to   60
oppose these insolences, which possibly yours may be too weak
to accomplish, to which end the council is ordered to meet this
evening, and desiring you will come and take your place there,
and be pleased to accept from us a commission to command
in chief in this war.—Therefore send those soldiers under your   65
command to their respective houses, and haste, sir, to your
affectionate friends.—"
FEARLESS. Sir, I fear the hearts and pen did not agree when this was
writ.
DARING. A plague upon their shallow politics! Do they think to play 70
the old game twice with us?
BACON. Away! You wrong the council, who of themselves are
honourable gentlemen, but the base coward fear of some of
them puts the rest on tricks that suit not with their nature.
DUNCE. Sir, 'tis for noble ends you're sent for, and for your safety I'll 75
engage my life.
DARING. By heaven and so you shall—and pay it too with all the
rest of your wise-headed council.

BACON. Your zeal is too officious now. I see no treachery and can
80   fear no danger.
DUNCE. Treachery! Now heavens forbid, are we not Christians sir,
        all friends and countrymen! Believe me sir, 'tis honour calls you
        to increase your fame, and he who would dissuade you is your
        enemy.
85 DARING. Go cant,[1] sir, to the rabble—for us—we know you.
BACON. You wrong me when you but suspect for me; let him that
        acts dishonourably fear. My innocence and my good sword's my
        guard.
DARING. If you resolve to go, we will attend you.
90 BACON. What, go like an invader? No Daring, the invitation's
        friendly, and as a friend, attended only by my menial servants,
        I'll wait upon the council that they may see that when I could
        command it I came a humble suppliant for their favour. You
        may return and tell them I'll attend.
95 DUNCE. I kiss your Honour's hands.

        (*Goes out.*)

DARING. 'Sdeath,[2] will you trust the faithless council, sir, who have
        so long held you in hand with promises, that curse of statesmen,
        that unlucky vice that renders even nobility despised?
BACON. Perhaps the council thought me too aspiring, and would
100   not add wings to my ambitious flight.
DARING. A pox of their considering caps, and now they find that
        you can soar alone, they send for you to nip your spreading
        wings. Now by my soul you shall not go alone.
BACON. Forbear, lest I suspect you for a mutineer; I am resolved to
105   go.
FEARLESS. What, and send your army home? A pretty fetch.
DARING. By heaven we'll not disband—not till we see how fairly
        you are dealt with: if you have a commission to be General, here
        we are ready to receive new orders. If not, we'll ring them such a
110   thundering peal shall beat the town about their treacherous ears.

---

1   *cant* Talk or argue in a way that involves insincere posturing.
2   *'Sdeath* Literally a short form of the phrase "God's death," meant as a curse.

BACON. I do command you not to stir a man till you're informed how I am treated by them. Leave me all.

(*Exeunt Officers.*)

(*While Bacon reads the letter again, to him the Indian Queen with women waiting.*)

QUEEN. Now while my lord's asleep in his pavilion I'll try my power with the General for an accommodation of a peace. The very dreams of war fright my soft slumbers that used to be employed   115
in kinder business.
BACON. Ha! The Queen! What happiness is this that presents itself which all my industry could never gain?
QUEEN. Sir—

(*Approaching him.*)

BACON. Pressed with the great extremities of joy and fear I trem-   120
bling stand, unable to approach her.
QUEEN. I hope you will not think it fear in me, though timorous as a dove by nature framed. Nor that my lord, whose youth's unskilled in war, can either doubt his courage or his forces that makes me seek a reconciliation on any honourable terms of   125
peace.
BACON. Ah madam! If you knew how absolutely you command my fate, I fear but little honour would be left me, since whatsoe'er you ask me I should grant.
QUEEN. Indeed I would not ask your honour, sir, that renders you   130
too brave in my esteem. Nor can I think that you would part with that. No, not to save your life.
BACON. I would do more to serve your least commands than part with trivial life.
QUEEN. Bless me! Sir, how came I by such a power?   135
BACON. The gods and Nature gave it to you in your creation, formed with all the charms that ever graced your sex.
QUEEN. Is it possible? Am I so beautiful?
BACON. As heaven or angels there.

140 QUEEN. Supposing this, how can my beauty make you so obliging?
BACON. Beauty has still a power over great souls, and from the
moment I beheld your eyes, my stubborn heart melted to
compliance, and from a nature rough and turbulent grew soft
and gentle as the god of love.
145 QUEEN. The god of love! what is the god of love?
BACON. 'Tis a resistless fire, that's kindled thus—(*Takes her by the
hand and gazes on her.*) At every gaze we take from fine eyes,
from such bashful looks, and such soft touches—it makes us
sigh—and pant as I do now, and stops the breath when e'er we
150 speak of pain.
QUEEN. (*Aside.*) Alas for me if this should be love!
BACON. It makes us tremble when we touch the fair one, and all the
blood runs shivering through the veins, the heart's surrounded
with a feeble languishment, the eyes are dying, and the cheeks
155 are pale, the tongue is faltering, and the body fainting.
QUEEN. (*Aside.*) Then I am undone, and all I feel is love. [*To Bacon.*]
If love be catching, sir, by looks and touches, let us at distance
parley—or rather let me fly, for within view, is too near—
BACON. (*Aside.*) Ah! She retires—Displeased I fear with my pre-
160 sumptuous love. (*To Semernia.*) Oh pardon, fairest creature!

(*Kneels.*)

QUEEN. I'll talk no more. Our words exchange our souls and
every look fades all my blooming honour, like sunbeams on
unguarded roses. Take all our kingdoms—make our people
slaves, and let me fall beneath your conquering sword. But never
165 let me hear you talk again or gaze upon your eyes. (*Goes out.*)
BACON. She loves! By heaven, she loves! And has not art enough
to hide her flame though she have cruel honour to suppress it.
However, I'll pursue her to the banquet. (*Exit.*)

ACT 2, SCENE 2

(*The Widow Ranter's hall. Enter Surelove, fanned by two Negroes,*[1] *followed by Hazard.*)

SURELOVE. This Madam Ranter is so prodigious a treater[2]—oh! I hate a room that smells of a great dinner, and what's worse, a dessert of punch and tobacco. What? Are you taking leave so soon, cousin?

HAZARD. Yes madam. But 'tis not fit I should let you know with   5
what regret I go. But business must be obeyed.

SURELOVE. Some letters to dispatch to English ladies you have left behind—come, cousin,[3] confess.

HAZARD. I own I much admire the English beauties, but never yet have put their fetters on.[4]   10

SURELOVE. Never in love—oh, then you have pleasures to come.

HAZARD. Rather a pain when there's no hope attends it.

SURELOVE. Oh, such diseases quickly cure themselves.

HAZARD. I do not wish to find it so; for even in pain I find a pleasure too.   15

SURELOVE. You are infected then, and came abroad for a cure.

HAZARD. Rather to receive my wounds, madam.

SURELOVE. Already sir—whoe'er she be, she made good haste to conquer. We have few here who boast that dexterity.

HAZARD. What think you of Chrisante, madam?   20

SURELOVE. (*Coldly.*) I must confess your love and your despair are there placed right, of which I am not fond of being made a confidant, since I am assured she can love none but Friendly.

HAZARD. Let her love on as long as life shall last. Let Friendly take her, and the universe, so I had my next wish. (*Sighs.*) Madam, it   25
is yourself that I adore. I should not be so vain to tell you this, but that I know you've found the secret out already from my sighs.

---

1   *two Negroes*   The earliest records attesting to the presence of enslaved Africans in Virginia date to 1619. Behn's Widow shows off her newly found wealth with opulent displays including both enslaved Africans and indentured servants from Scotland who serve and entertain her guests.

2   *treater*   Entertainer of guests.

3   *cousin*   Term of affection used for friends as well as relatives.

4   *put their fetters on*   I.e., married.

30 SURELOVE. Forbear sir, and know me for your kinsman's wife and no more.

HAZARD. Be scornful as you please, rail at my passion and refuse to hear it, yet I'll love on, and hope in spite of you, my flame shall be so constant and submissive it shall compel your heart to some return.

35 SURELOVE. You're very confident of your power, I perceive, but if you chance to find yourself mistaken, say your opinion and your affectation were misapplied and not that I was cruel.

(*Exit Surelove.*)

HAZARD. Whate'er denials dwell upon your tongue, your eyes assure me that your heart is tender. (*Goes out.*)

(*Enter the Bagpiper playing before a great bowl of punch, carried between two Negroes, a Highlander dancing after it, the Widow Ranter led by Timorous, Chrisante by Dullman; Mrs. Flirt and Friendly all dancing after it; they place it on the table.*)

40 DULLMAN. This is like the noble widow all over, i'faith.

TIMOROUS. Aye, aye, the widow's health in a full-ladle, Major. (*Drinks.*) But a pox on't, what made that young fellow here that affronted us yesterday, Major? (*While they drink about.*)

DULLMAN. Some damned sharper that would lay his knife aboard[1]

45 your Widow Cornet.

TIMOROUS. Zoors, if I thought so, I'd arrest him for salt and battery, lay him in prison for a swinging fine,[2] and take no bail!

DULLMAN. Nay, had it not been before my mistress here, Mistress Chrisante, I had swinged him for his yesterday's affront! Ah, my

50 sweet Mistress Chrisante—if you did but know what a power you have over me.

CHRISANTE. Oh, you're a great courtier, Major.

DULLMAN. Would I were anything for your sake, madam.

---

1 *sharper* Rogue or cheater; *lay his knife aboard* Phrase that means to settle in for a meal, but carries a sexual connotation as well.

2 *salt and battery* Malapropism for "assault and battery"; *swinging fine* Penalty by hanging.

RANTER. Thou art anything but what thou shouldst be; prithee
Major, leave off being an old buffoon—that is, a lover turned to   55
ridicule by age—consider thyself a mere rolling tun[1] of Nants—
a walking chimney, ever smoking with nasty mundungus[2]—and
then thou hast a countenance like an old worm-eaten cheese.
DULLMAN. Well, Widow, you will joke—ha, ha, ha—
TIMOROUS. Gadzoors, she's pure company—ha, ha—   60
DULLMAN. No matter for my countenance. Colonel Downright
likes my estate and is resolved to have it a match.
FRIENDLY. Dear Widow, take off your damned Major, for if he speak
another word to Chrisante, I shall be put past all my patience
and fall foul upon him.   65
RANTER. S'life,[3] not for the world—Major, I bar love-making[4]
within my territories. 'Tis inconsistent with the punch bowl. If
you'll drink, do, if not, be gone!
TIMOROUS. Nay, gadzooks, if you enter me at the punch bowl, you
enter me in politics. Well, 'tis the best drink in Christendom for   70
a statesman. (*They drink about, the bagpipe playing.*)
RANTER. Come, now you shall see what my Highland varlet[5] can
do—(*A Scot's dance.*)
DULLMAN. So—I see. Let the world go which way it will. Widow,
you are resolved for mirth. But come—to the conversation of   75
the times.
RANTER. The times? Why the devil ails the times? I see nothing in
the times but a company of coxcombs that fear without a cause.
TIMOROUS. But if these fears were laid and Bacon were hanged, I
look upon Virginia to be the happiest part of the world, gad-   80
zoors. Why there's England—'tis nothing to it. I was in England
about six years ago and it showed the Court of Aldermen,[6] some
were nodding, some saying nothing, and others very little to

---

1   *tun*   Cask.
2   *mundungus*   Cheap tobacco.
3   *S'life*   Short for "God's life," meant as a curse (similar to "God's death," above).
4   *love-making*   Courtship or flirtation (not necessarily with an implication of sexual
    intercourse).
5   *varlet*   Personal attendant.
6   *Court of Aldermen*   Municipal council consisting of representatives from the various
    neighborhoods in London.

85   purpose. But how could it be otherwise? For they had neither
      bowl of punch, bottles of wine or tobacco for the young gentle-
      men. Their farthest travels is to France or Italy—they never
      come hither.

DULLMAN. The more's the pity by my troth. (*Drinks.*)

TIMOROUS. Where they learn to swear, mor-blew, mor-dee.[1]

90 FRIENDLY. And tell you how much bigger the Louvre is than White-
      hall; buy a suit a-la-mode,[2] get a swinging cap of[3] some French
      marquis, spend all their money and return just as they went.

DULLMAN. For the old fellows, their business is usury, extortion,
      and undermining young heirs.

95 TIMOROUS. Then for young merchants, their Exchange is the tavern,
      their warehouse the playhouse, and their bills of exchange *billet-
      doux*,[4] where to sup with their wenches at the other end of the
      town. Now judge you what a condition poor England is in: for
      my part I look upon it as a lost nation, gadzoors.

100 DULLMAN. I have considered it and have found a way to save all yet.

TIMOROUS. As how I pray?

DULLMAN. As thus: we have men here of great experience and
      ability—now I would have as many sent into England as would
      supply all places and offices, both civil and military, d'ye see?

105   Their young gentry should all travel hither for breeding and to
      learn the mysteries of state.

FRIENDLY. As for the old covetous fellows, I would have the trades-
      men get in their debts, break and turn troopers.[5]

TIMOROUS. And they'd be soon weary of extortion, gadzoors.

110 DULLMAN. Then for the young merchants, there should be a law
      made: none should go beyond Ludgate.[6]

---

1   *mor-blew, mor-dee*   Timorous is mocking French curses *morbleu* and *mordieu*.

2   *the Louvre*   In the seventeenth century, the Parisian residence of the French monar-
    chy; *Whitehall*   In seventeenth-century London, the primary residence of the English
    monarch; *a-la-mode*   Fashionable; Paris had, by the mid-seventeenth century, acquired
    a reputation for being a center of European fashion.

3   *get a swinging cap of*   The meaning of this idiomatic phrase is unclear; it may mean
    something like "get the better of."

4   *billet-doux*   French: love note(s).

5   *troopers*   Soldiers in a horse regiment.

6   *Ludgate*   Originally a low-security prison for debtors and other minor offenses, but in the
    seventeenth century, it was a street occupied primarily by merchants.

FRIENDLY. You have found out the only way to preserve that great kingdom. (*Drinking all this while sometimes.*)

TIMOROUS. Well, gadzoors, 'tis a fine thing to be a good statesman.

FRIENDLY. Aye, Cornet, which you had never been had you stayed in old England. 115

DULLMAN. Why, sir, we were somebody in England.

FRIENDLY. So I heard, Major.

DULLMAN. You heard, sir? What have you heard? He's a kidnapper[1] that says he heard anything of me—and so my service to you— 120 I'll sue you, sir, for spoiling my marriage here by your scandals with Mrs. Chrisante. But that shan't do sir. I'll marry her for all that, and he's a rascal that denies it.

FRIENDLY. S'death you lie, sir—I do.

TIMOROUS. Gadzoors sir, lie to a Privy Counsellor, a Major of 125 Horse![2] Brother, this is an affront to our dignities. Draw[3] and I'll side with you. (*They both draw on Friendly; the ladies run off.*)

FRIENDLY. If I disdain to draw, 'tis not that I fear your base and cowardly force, but for the respect I bear you as magistrates. And so, I leave you. (*Goes out.*) 130

TIMOROUS. An arrant coward, gadzoors.

DULLMAN. A mere poltroon,[4] and I scorn to drink in his company.

(*Exeunt, putting up their swords.*)

ACT 2, SCENE 3

(*A savannah or a large heath.*)

(*Enter Whimsey, Whiff, and Boozer, with some soldiers, armed.*)

WHIMSEY. Stand—stand—and hear the word of command. Do ye see yon copse, and that ditch that runs along Major Dullman's plantation?

---

1 *kidnapper* Here suggests any person of ill-repute.
2 *Major of Horse* Officer in the cavalry.
3 *Draw* I.e., draw your sword.
4 *poltroon* Worthless coward.

BOOZER. We do.

5 WHIMSEY. Place your men there, and lie flat on your bellies. When Bacon comes (if alone), seize him, d'ye see?

WHIFF. Observe the command now (if alone), for we are not for bloodshed.

BOOZER. I'll warrant you for our parts.

(*Exuent all but Whimsey and Whiff.*)

10 WHIMSEY. Now we have ambushed our men, let's light our pipes and sit down and take an encouraging dram of the bottle. (*Pulls a bottle of brandy out of his pocket—they sit.*)

WHIFF. Thou art a knave and hast emptied half the bottle in thy leathern pockets. But come, here's young Frightall's health.

15 WHIMSEY. What, wilt drink a man's health thou'rt going to hang?

WHIFF. 'Tis all one for that. We'll drink his health first and hang him afterwards, and thou shalt pledge me d'ye see and though 'twere under the gallows.

WHIMSEY. Thou art a traitor for saying so and I defy thee.

20 WHIFF. Nay, since we are come out like loving brothers to hang the general, let's not fall out among ourselves. And so here's to you [*drinks*] though I have no great maw[1] to this business.

WHIMSEY. Prithee brother Whiff, do not be so villainous a coward, for I hate a coward.

25 WHIFF. Nay, 'tis not that, but my Whiff, my Nancy dreamt tonight she saw me hanged.

WHIMSEY. 'Twas a cowardly dream—think no more on it, but as dreams are expounded by contraries, thou shalt hang the general.

WHIFF. Aye—but he was my friend, and I owe him at this time a
30 hundred pounds of tobacco.

WHIMSEY. Nay, then I'm sure thou'dst hang him if he were thy brother.

WHIFF. But hark—I think I hear the neighing of horses. Where shall we hide ourselves? If we stay here, we shall be mauled
35 damnably.

---

1   *maw* Belly; i.e., appetite or liking.

(*Exeunt both behind a bush, peeping.*)

(*Enter Bacon, Fearless, and three or four footmen.*)

BACON. Let the groom lead the horses o'er the savannah. We'll walk
it on foot. It's not a quarter of a mile to the town and here the
air is cool.
FEARLESS. The breezes about this time of day begin to take wing and
fan refreshment to the trees and flowers.   40
BACON. And at these hours how fragrant are the groves.
FEARLESS. The country's well, were but the people so.
BACON. But come, let's on—

(*They tell pass to the entrance.*)

WHIMSEY. There, boys!

(*The soldiers come forth and fall on Bacon.*)

BACON. Ha! Ambush!   45

(*Draws. Fearless and the footmen draw, the soldiers after a while
fighting take Bacon and Fearless, they having laid three or four dead.*)

WHIFF. So, so. He's taken. Now we may venture out.
WHIMSEY. But are you sure he's taken?
WHIFF. Sure, can't you believe your eyes? Come forth, I hate a
coward. Oh sir, have we caught your Mightiness?
BACON. Are you the authors of this valiant act? None but such   50
villainous cowards durst have attempted it.
WHIMSEY. Stop his railing tongue.
WHIFF. No, no. Let him rail. Let him rail now his hands are tied,
ha ha! Why, good General Frightall, what, was nobody able d'ye
think to tame the roaring lion?   55
BACON. You'll be hanged for this!
WHIMSEY. Come, come. Away with him to the next tree.
BACON. What mean you villains?

WHIFF. Only to hang your Honour a little, that's all. We'll teach
60   you, sir, to serve your country against law.

(*As they go off, enter Daring with soldiers.*)

DARING. Hah! My general betrayed! This I suspected.

(*His men come in, they fall on, release Bacon and Fearless and his
man, who get swords. Whimsey's party put Whimsey and Whiff before
them, striking them as they endeavour to run on this side or that, and
forcing them to bear up. They are taken after some fighting.*)

FEARLESS. Did not the general tell you rogues you'd all be hanged?
WHIFF. Oh, Nancy, Nancy, how prophetic are thy dreams!
BACON. Come, let's on—
65 DARING. 'Sdeath, what mean you sir?
BACON. As I designed—to present myself to the council.
DARING. By heavens! We'll follow then to save you from their
        treachery. 'Twas this that has befallen you that I feared, which
        made me at a distance follow you.
70 BACON. Follow me still, but still at such distance as your aids may
        be assisting on all occasion. Fearless, go back and bring your
        regiment down, and Daring, let your sergeant with his party
        guard these villains to the council.

(*Exeunt Bacon, Daring, and Fearless.*)

WHIFF. A pox on your Worship's plot.
75 WHIMSEY. A pox on your forwardness to come out of the hedge.

(*Exeunt officers with Whimsey and Whiff.*)

ACT 2, SCENE 4

(*The council table.*)

(*Enter Colonel Wellman, Colonel Downright, Dullman, Timorous,
and about seven or eight more seat themselves.*)

WELLMAN. You heard Mr. Dunce's opinion, gentlemen, concerning Bacon's coming upon our invitation. He believes he will come, but I rather think, though he be himself undaunted, yet the persuasions of his two lieutenant generals, Daring and Fearless, may prevent him—Colonel, have you ordered our men to be in arms?   5

(*Enter a soldier.*)

DOWNRIGHT. I have, and they'll attend further order on the savannah.
SOLDIER. May it please your Honours, Bacon is on his way. He comes unattended by any but his footmen and Colonel Fearless.   10
DOWNRIGHT. Who is this fellow?
WELLMAN. A spy I sent to watch Bacon's motions.
SOLDIER. But there is a company of soldiers in ambush on this side of the savannah to seize him as he passes by.
WELLMAN. That's by no order of the council.   15
ALL. No, no, no order.
WELLMAN. Nay, 'twere a good design if true.
TIMOROUS. Gadzoors, would I had thought on't for my troop.
DOWNRIGHT. I am for no unfair dealing in any extremity.

(*Enter a messenger [Brag] in haste.*)

BRAG. An't please your Honours, the saddest news: An ambush   20
being laid for Bacon, they rushed out upon him on the savannah, and after some fighting, took him and Fearless—
TIMOROUS. Is this your sad news? Zoors, would I had had a hand in it.
BRAG. When on a sudden, Daring and his party fell in upon us,   25
turned the tide, killed our men and took Capitan Whimsey and Capitan Whiff prisoners, the rest run away, but Bacon fought like a fury.
TIMOROUS. A bloody fellow.
DOWNRIGHT. Whimsey and Whiff? They deserve death for acting   30
without order!

TIMOROUS. I am of the colonel's opinion; they deserve to hang for
it.

DULLMAN. Why, brother, I thought you had wished the plot had
35 been yours but now?

TIMOROUS. Aye, but the case is altered since that, good brother.

WELLMAN. Now he's exasperated past all hopes of a reconciliation.

DULLMAN. You must make use of the statesman's refuge: wise
dissimulation.

40 BRAG. For all this, sir, he will not believe but that you mean honour-
ably, and no persuasions could hinder him from coming, so he
has dismissed all his soldiers and is entering the town on foot.

WELLMAN. What pity 'tis a brave man should be guilty of an ill
action.

45 BRAG. But the noise of his danger has so won the hearts of the
mobile[1] that they increase his train as he goes and follow him in
the town like a victor.

WELLMAN. Go wait his coming. He grows too popular and must be
humbled.

(Exit Brag.)

50 TIMOROUS. I was ever of your mind, Colonel.

WELLMAN. Aye, right or wrong—but what's your counsel now?

TIMOROUS. Even as it used to be. I leave it to wiser heads.

(Enter Brag.)

BRAG. Bacon, sir, is entering.

TIMOROUS. Gadzoors, would I were safe in bed.

55 DULLMAN. Colonel, keep in your heat and treat calmly with him.

WELLMAN. I rather wish you would all follow me. I'd meet him at
the head of all this noisy rabble and seize him from the rout.

DOWNRIGHT. What men of authority dispute with rakehells?[2] 'Tis
below us, sir.

60 TIMOROUS. To stake our lives and fortunes against their nothing.

---

1   *mobile*   Populace; rabble
2   *rakehells*   Scoundrels.

(*Enter Bacon, after him the rabble with staves and clubs bringing in Whimsey and Whiff, bound.*)

WELLMAN. What means this insolence? What—Mr. Bacon, do you come in arms?

BACON. I'd need, sir, to come in arms, when men that should be honourable can have so poor designs to take my life.

WELLMAN. Thrust out his following rabble.   65

FIRST RABBLE. We'll not stir till we have the general safe back again.

BACON. Let not your loves be too officious—but retire—

FIRST RABBLE. At your command, we vanish. (*The rabble retire.*)

BACON. I hope you'll pardon me if in my own defense I seized on these two murderers.   70

DOWNRIGHT. You did well, sir. 'Twas by no order they acted. Stand forth, and hear your sentence! In time of war we need no formal trials to hang knaves that act without order.

WHIFF. Oh mercy, mercy, Colonel! 'Twas Parson Dunce's plot!

DOWNRIGHT. Issue out a warrant to seize Dunce immediately. You   75
shall be carried to the fort to pray.

WHIMSEY. Oh good, your Honour, I never prayed in all my life.

DOWNRIGHT. From thence drawn upon a sledge to the place of execution where you shall hang till you are dead, and then be cut down and ...   80

WHIMSEY. Oh hold, hold! We shall never be able to endure half of this. (*Kneeling.*)

WELLMAN. I think the offense needs not so great a punishment. Their crime, sir, is but equal to your own: acting without commission.   85

BACON. 'Tis very well explained, sir. Had I been murdered by commission then, the deed had been approved, and now, perhaps, I am beholding to the rabble for my life.

WELLMAN. A fine pretence to hide a popular fault. But for this once, we pardon them and you.   90

BACON. Pardon? For what? By heaven, I scorn your pardon. I've not offended honour nor religion.

WELLMAN. You've offended both in taking arms.

BACON. Should I stand by and see my country ruined, my king dishonoured, and his subjects murdered, hear the sad cries of   95

widows and orphans? You heard it loud, but gave no pitying
care to it. And till the war and massacre was brought to my own
door, my flocks and herds surprised, I bore it all with patience.
Is it unlawful to defend myself against a thief that breaks into
100   my doors?
WELLMAN. And call you this defending of yourself?
BACON. I call it doing of myself that right which upon just demand
the council did refuse me. If my ambition, as you're pleased to
call it, made me demand too much, I left myself to you.
105 WELLMAN. Perhaps we thought it did.
BACON. Sir, you affront my birth. I am a gentleman, and yet my
thoughts were humble. I would have fought under the meanest
of your parasites—
TIMOROUS. (*To Dullman.*) There's a bob[1] for us, brother.
110 BACON. But still you put me off with promises. And when compelled to stir in my defense I called none to my aid, and those
that came, 'twas their own wrongs that urged them.
DOWNRIGHT. 'Tis feared, sir, under this pretense you aim at
government.
115 BACON. I scorn to answer to so base an accusation. The height of my
ambition is to be an honest subject.
WELLMAN. An honest rebel, sir.
BACON. You know you wrong me, and 'tis basely urged—but this
is trifling—here are my commissions. (*Throws down papers.*
120   *Downright reads.*)
DOWNRIGHT. To be general of the forces against the Indians and
blank commissions for his friends.
WELLMAN. Tear them in pieces! Are we to be imposed upon? Do
you come in hostile manner to compel us?
125 DOWNRIGHT. Be not too rough, sir. Let us argue with him.
WELLMAN. I am resolved I will not.
TIMOROUS. Then we are all dead men, gadzoors! He will not give us
time to say our prayers.
WELLMAN. We every day expect fresh force from England. Till then,
130   we of ourselves shall be sufficient to make defense against a
sturdy traitor.

---

1   *bob* Shilling. Timorous suggests that by "parasites," Bacon is referring to him and
Dullman.

BACON. Traitor! 'Sdeath! Traitor? I defy ye, but that my honour's yet above my anger, I'd make you answer me that traitor dearly.

(*Rises.*)

WELLMAN. Hah! Am I threatened? Guards! Secure the rebel.

(*Guards seize him.*)

BACON. Is this your honourable invitation? Go—triumph in your   135
short-lived victory. The next turn shall be mine.

(*Exeunt guards with Bacon.*)

(*A noise of fighting—enter Bacon, Wellman, his guards beaten back by the rabble, Bacon snatches a sword from one, and keeps back the rabble. Timorous gets under the table.*)

DOWNRIGHT. What means this insolence?
RABBLE. We'll have our general, and knock that fellow's brains out, and hang up Colonel Wellman!
ALL. Aye! Aye! Hang up Wellman!   140

(*The rabble seize Wellman, and Dullman, and the rest.*)

DULLMAN. Hold, hold, gentlemen! I was always for the general.
RABBLE. Let's barbeque¹ this fat rogue!
BACON. Be gone, and know your distance to the council.

(*The rabble let them go.*)

WELLMAN. (*In rage.*) I'd rather perish by the meanest hand than owe my safety poorly thus to Bacon.   145
BACON. If you persist still in that mind I'll leave you, and conquering, make you happy against your will.

---

1 *barbeque* Spelled "barbicu" in the original text, this is among the earliest known appearances of the word in English.

(*Exeunt Bacon and rabble, hollowing, "A Bacon! A Bacon!"*)

WELLMAN. Oh villainous cowards. Who will trust his honour with
sycophants so base? Let us to arms! By heaven, I will not give my
150 body rest till I've chastised the boldness of this rebel.

(*Exuent Wellman, Downright, and the rest, all but Dullman.
Timorous peeps from under the table.*)

TIMOROUS. What, is the roistering hector[1] gone, brother?
DULLMAN. Aye, aye. And the devil go with him!

(*Looking sadly, Timorous comes out.*)

TIMOROUS. Was there ever such a bull of Bashan?[2] Why, what if he
should come down upon us and kill us all for traitors?
155 DULLMAN. I rather think the council will hang us all for cowards—
ah—oh—a drum—a drum—oh! (*He goes out.*)
TIMOROUS. This is the misery of being great,
We're sacrificed to every turn of state.

[*Exeunt.*]

ACT 3, SCENE I

(*The country court, a great table, with papers, a clerk writing. Enter a
great many people of all sorts, then Friendly, after him Dullman.*)

FRIENDLY. How now, Major? What, they say Bacon scared you all
out of the council yesterday. What say the people?
DULLMAN. Say? They curse us all, and drink young Frightall's
health, and swear they'll fight through brimstone for him.
5 FRIENDLY. And tomorrow they will hallow him to the gallows if it
were his chance to come there.
DULLMAN. 'Tis very likely. Why, I am forced to be guarded to the

---

1 *roistering hector* Riotous bully.
2 *bull of Bashan* See Psalm 22.12: "Strong bulls of Bashan have beset me round."

court now, the rabble swear they would De Wit[1] me, but I shall
hamper some of them. Would the governor were here to bear
the brunt of it, for they call us the Evil Counsellors.   10

(*Enter Hazard, goes to Friendly.*)

Here's the young rogue that drew upon us too. We have rods
and piss[2] for him i'faith.

(*Enter Timorous with bailiffs; whispers to Dullman, after which to
the bailiffs.*)

TIMOROUS. Gadzoors that's he! Do your office.
BAILIFF. We arrest you, sir, in the king's name, at the suit of the
    Honourable Justice Timorous.   15
HAZARD. Justice Timorous? Who the devil is he?
TIMOROUS. I am the man, sir, d'ye see, for want of a better. You shall
    repent, gadzoors, your putting of tricks upon persons of my
    rank and quality.

(*After he has spoken he runs back as [if] afraid of him.*)

HAZARD. Your rank and quality!   20
TIMOROUS. Aye, sir, my rank and quality. First, I am one of the
    honourable council; next, Justice of the Peace in Corum, Cornet
    of a Troop of Horse, d'ye see, and Churchwarden.
FRIENDLY. From whence proceeds this Mr. Justice, you said nothing
    of this at Madam Ranter's yesterday. You saw him there, then   25
    you were good friends?
TIMOROUS. Aye, however I have carried my body swimmingly
    before my mistress, d'ye see. I had rancor in my heart, gadzoors.
FRIENDLY. Why, this gentleman's a stranger and but lately come
    ashore.   30

---

1 *De Wit* Reference to Johann De Witt (1625–72), Dutch politician known for his opposi-
   tion to the ruling group; he was ultimately killed by a pro-monarchy mob.
2 *rods and piss* A "rod" is a stick used for punishment; combining rods and "piss" suggests
   the addition of urine into the reprimand.

HAZARD. At my first landing I was in company with this fellow
and two or three of his cruel brethren, where I was affronted by
them, some words passed, and I drew.

TIMOROUS. Aye, aye, sir, you shall pay for it—why—what sir,
35   cannot a civil magistrate affront a man, but he must be drawn
upon presently?

FRIENDLY. Well sir, the gentleman shall answer your suit, and I hope
you'll take my bail for him.

TIMOROUS. 'Tis enough. I know you to be a civil person.

(*Timorous and Dullman take their places, on a long bench placed
behind the table; to them Whimsey and Whiff, they seat themselves,
then Boozer and two or three more who seat themselves, then enter two
bearing a bowl of punch and a great ladle or two in it; the rest of the
stage being filled with people.*)

40   WHIFF. Brothers, it has been often moved at the bench that a new
punch bowl should be provided, and one of larger circumfer-
ence, when the bench sits late about weighty affairs. Oftentimes
the bowl is emptied before we end.

WHIMSEY. A good motion. Clerk, set it down.

45   CLERK. Mr. Justice Boozer, the council has ordered you a writ of
ease[1] and dismissed your Worship from the bench.

BOOZER. Me from the bench? For what?

WHIMSEY. The complaint is, Brother Boozer, for drinking too much
punch in the time of hearing trials.

50   WHIFF. And that you can neither write nor read, nor say the Lord's
Prayer.

TIMOROUS. That your warrants are like a brewer's tally, a notch on
a stick;[2] if a special warrant, then a couple. Gadzoors, when his
Excellency comes, he will have no such justices.

55   BOOZER. Why, brother, though I can't read myself, I have had
Dalton's *Country Justice*[3] read to me two or three times, and

---

1   *writ of ease*   Certificate of dismissal.
2   *brewer's ... stick*   Beer tab kept by making marks on a stick.
3   *Dalton's Country Justice*   Widely referenced 1618 book about legal matters by Michael
    Dalton, popular throughout the seventeenth century.

understand the law. This is your malice, Brother Whiff, because my wife does not come to your warehouse to buy her commodities. But no matter. To show I have no malice in my heart, I drink your health. I care not this. I turn lawyer and plead at the Board. (*Drinks; all pledge him and hum.*) 60

DULLMAN. Mr. Clerk, come, to the trials on the docket.

(*Clerk reads.*)

CLERK. The first is between his Worship Justice Whiff and one Grubb.

DULLMAN. Aye, that Grubb's a common disturber. Brother, your cause is a good cause if well managed. Here's to it. (*Drinks.*) 65

WHIFF. I thank you, brother Dullman. Read my petition. (*Drinks.*)

CLERK. "The Petition of Capitan Thomas Whiff showeth, whereas Gilbert Grubb calls his worship's wife Ann Whiff a whore, and said he would prove it; your Petitioner desires the Worshipful Bench to take it into consideration, and your Petitioner shall pray, etc." Here's two witnesses have made affidavit *viva voce*[1] an't like your Worships. 70

DULLMAN. Call Grubb.

CLERK. Gilbert Grubb, come into the court. 75

GRUBB. Here.

WHIMSEY. Well, what can you say for yourself, Mr. Grubb?

GRUBB. Why, an't like your Worship, my wife invited some neighbors' wives to drink a keg of cider; now your Worship's wife Madam Whiff, being there fuddled,[2] would have thrust me out of doors and bid me go to my old whore Madam Whimsey, (*To Whimsey.*) meaning your Worship's wife. 80

WHIMSEY. Hah! My wife called whore! She's a jade and I'll arrest her husband here in an action of debts.

TIMOROUS. Gadzoors, she's no better than she should be, I'll warrant her. 85

WHIFF. Look ye, brother Whimsey, be patient. You know the humour of my Nancy when she's drunk, but when she's sober,

---

1 *viva voce* Latin: in person.
2 *fuddled* I.e., befuddled; drunk.

she's a civil person, and shall ask your pardon.

90 WHIMSEY. Let this be done and I am satisfied. And so here's to you. (*Drinks.*)

DULLMAN. Go on to the trial.

GRUBB. I being very angry, said, indeed, I would prove her a greater whore than Madam Whimsey.

95 CLERK. An't like your Worships, he confesses the words in open court.

GRUBB. Why, an't like your Worships, she has had two bastards. I'll prove it.

WHIFF. Sirrah, sirrah, that was when she was a maid, not since I

100 married her. My marrying her made her honest.

DULLMAN. Let there be an order of the court to sue him for *Scandalum Magnatum.*

TIMOROUS. Mr. Clerk, let my cause come next.

CLERK. The defendant's ready, sir.

(*Hazard comes to the board.*)

105 TIMOROUS. Brothers of the Bench take notice that this hector here coming into Mrs. Flirt's ordinary where I was with my brothers Dullman and Lieutenant Boozer, we gave him good counsel to fall to work. Now my gentleman here was affronted at this forsooth, and makes no more to do but calls us scoundrels and

110 drew his sword on us, and had I not defended myself by running away, he had murdered me and assassinated my two brothers.

WHIFF. What witness have you, brother?

TIMOROUS. Here's Mrs. Flirt and her maid Nell—besides we may be witness for one another I hope, our words may be taken.

115 CLERK. Mrs. Flirt and Nell are sworn.

(*They stand forth.*)

WHIMSEY. By the oaths that you have taken, speak nothing but the truth.

FLIRT. An't please your Worships, your Honours came to my house, where you found this young gentleman; and your Honours

120 invited him to drink with your Honours, where after some

opprobrious words given him, Justice Dullman and Justice
Boozer struck him over the head; and after that, indeed the
gentleman drew.

TIMOROUS. Mark that, brother, he drew.

HAZARD. If I did, it was *de defendendo*.[1]   125

TIMOROUS. Do you hear that, brothers? He did it in defiance.

HAZARD. Sir, you ought not to sit judge and accuser too.

WHIFF. The gentleman's in the right, brother, you cannot do it
according to the law.

TIMOROUS. Gadzoors, what new tricks, new quirks?   130

HAZARD. Gentlemen, take notice. He swears in court.

TIMOROUS. Gadzoors, what's that to you, sir?

HAZARD. This is the second time of his swearing.

WHIMSEY. What do you think we are deaf, sir? Come, come.
Proceed.   135

TIMOROUS. I desire he may be bound to his good behaviour, fined
and deliver up his sword. What say you, brother? (*Jogs Dullman,
who nods.*)

WHIMSEY. He's asleep. Drink to him and waken him. You have
missed the cause by sleeping, brother. (*Drinks.*)   140

DULLMAN. Justice may nod, but never sleeps, brother. You were at
"deliver his sword"—a good motion. Let it be done. (*Drinks.*)

HAZARD. No, gentlemen. I wear a sword to right myself.

TIMOROUS. That's fine i'faith, gadzoors. I have worn a sword this
dozen year and never could right myself.   145

WHIFF. Aye, 'twould be a fine world if men should wear swords to
right themselves. He that's bound to the peace shall wear no
sword.

WHIMSEY. I say he that's bound to the peace ought to wear no
peruke.[2] They may change 'em for black or white, and then who 150
can know them?

HAZARD. I hope, gentlemen, I may be allowed to speak for myself.

WHIFF. Aye, what can you say for yourself? Did you not draw your
sword, sirrah?

HAZARD. I did.   155

---

1 *de defendendo* Latin: in self defense.
2 *peruke* Periwig; i.e., a lawyer's wig.

TIMOROUS. 'Tis sufficient he confesses the fact, and we'll hear no
    more.

HAZARD. You will not hear the provocation given.

DULLMAN. 'Tis enough, sir, you drew.

160 WHIMSEY. Aye, aye, 'tis enough he drew. Let him be fined.

FRIENDLY. The gentleman should be heard. He's a kinsman too—to
    Colonel John Surelove.

TIMOROUS. Hum—Colonel Surelove's kinsman.

WHIFF. Is he so? Nay, then all the reason in the world he should be
165   heard, brothers.

WHIMSEY. Come, come Cornet. You shall be friends with the
    gentleman. This was some drunken bout, I'll reckon.

TIMOROUS. Ha ha ha! So it was, gadzoors.

WHIFF. Come, drink to the gentleman and put it up.

170 TIMOROUS. Sir, my service to you. I am heartily sorry for what's
    past, but it was in my drink. (*Drinks.*)

WHIMSEY. You hear his acknowledgements, sir, and when he is
    sober, he never quarrels. Come sir, sit down. My service to you.

HAZARD. I beg your excuse, gentlemen. I have earnest business.

175 DULLMAN. Let us adjourn the court and prepare to meet the regi-
    ments on the savannah.

(*All go but Friendly and Hazard.*)

HAZARD. Is this the best Court of Judicature your country affords?

FRIENDLY. To give it its due it is not. But how does thy amour
    thrive?

180 HAZARD. As well as I can wish in so short a time.

FRIENDLY. I see she regards thee with kind eyes, sighs, and blushes.

HAZARD. Yes, and tells me I am so like a brother she had—to excuse
    her kind concern—then blush[es] so prettily, that gad I could
    not forbear making a discovery of my heart.

185 FRIENDLY. Have a care of that. Come upon her by slow degrees, for
    I know she is virtuous. But come, let's to the savannah where I'll
    present you to the two colonels, Wellman and Downright, the
    men that manage all till the arrival of the governor.

[*Exeunt.*]

ACT 3, SCENE 2

(*The savannah or heath.*)

(*Enter Wellman, Downright, Boozer, and Officers.*)

WELLMAN. Have you dispatched the scouts to watch the motions
of the enemies? I know that Bacon's violent and haughty and
will resent our vain attempts upon him; therefore, we must be
speedy in prevention.

DOWNRIGHT. What forces have you raised since our last order? 5

BOOZER. Here is a list of them. They came but slowly in until we
promised everyone a bottle of brandy.

(*Enter Officer and Dunce.*)

OFFICER. We have brought Mr. Dunce here as your Honour commanded us. After strict search, we found him this morning in
bed with Madam Flirt. 10

DOWNRIGHT. No matter, he'll exclaim no less against the vices of
the flesh next Sunday.

DUNCE. I hope, sir, you will not credit the malice of my enemies.

WELLMAN. No more. You are free, and what you counselled about
the ambush was both prudent and seasonable, and perhaps I 15
now wish it had taken effect.

(*Enter Friendly and Hazard.*)

FRIENDLY. I have brought an English gentleman to kiss your hands,
sir, and offer you his service. He is young and brave, and kinsman to Colonel Surelove.

WELLMAN. Sir, you are welcome, and to let you see you are so, we 20
will give you your kinsman's command, captain of a troop of
horse-guards, which I am sure will be continued to you when
the governor arrives.

HAZARD. I shall endeavour to deserve the honour, sir.

(*Enter Dullman, Timorous, Whimsey, and Whiff, all in buff, scarf, and feather.*)[1]

25 DOWNRIGHT. So, gentlemen, I see you are in readiness.

TIMOROUS. Readiness! What means he? I hope we are not to be drawn out to go against the enemy, Major?

DULLMAN. If we are, they shall look a new Major for me.

WELLMAN. We were debating, gentlemen, what course were best to
30 pursue against this powerful rebel.

FRIENDLY. Why, sir, we have forces enough. Let's charge him instantly, delays are dangerous.

TIMOROUS. Why, what a damned fiery fellow's this!

DOWNRIGHT. But if we drive him to extremities, we fear his siding
35 with the Indians.

DULLMAN. Colonel Downright has hit it; why should we endanger our men against a desperate termagant?[2] If he love wounds and scars so well, let him exercise on our enemies—but if he will needs fall upon us, 'tis then time for us enough to venture our
40 lives and fortunes.

TIMOROUS. How, we go to Bacon? Under favour I think 'tis his duty to come to us, and you go to that, gadzoors.

FRIENDLY. If he do, 'twill cost you dear, I doubt, Cornet. I find by our list, sir, we are four thousand men.

45 TIMOROUS. Gadzoors, not enough for a breakfast for that insatiate Bacon, and his two lieutenant-generals Fearless and Daring.

(*Whiff sits on the ground with a bottle of brandy.*)

WHIMSEY. A morsel, a morsel.

WELLMAN. I am for an attack. What say you gentlemen to an attack? What, silent all? What say you, Major?

50 DULLMAN. I say, sir, I hope my courage was never in dispute. But sir, I am going to marry Colonel Downright's daughter here, and should I be slain in this battle, 'twould break her heart. Besides,

---

1 *buff, scarf, and feather* Presumably indicating military garb meant to imitate that of the Indigenous warriors.

2 *termagant* Quarrelsome or violent person.

sir, I should lose her fortune— (*Speaks big.*)[1]

WELLMAN. (*To Whimsey.*) Well, I'm sure here's a captain will never
flinch.   55

WHIMSEY. Who, I, an't like your Honour?

WELLMAN. Aye, you.

WHIMSEY. Who, I? Ha, ha, ha. Why, did your Honour think that I
would fight?

WELLMAN. Fight? Yes. Why else do you take commissions?   60

WHIMSEY. Commissions? O Lord, O Lord, take commissions
to fight! Ha, ha, ha! That's a jest, if all that take commissions
should fight!

WELLMAN. Why do you bear arms then?

WHIMSEY. Why, for the pay. And to be called Captain, noble   65
Captain, to show, to cock and look big and bluff[2] as I do; to
be bowed to thus as we pass, to domineer, and beat our soldiers.
Fight, quoth he, ha ha hah!

FRIENDLY. But what makes you look so simply, Cornet?

TIMOROUS. Why, a thing that I have quite forgot. All my accounts   70
for England are to be made up, and I'm undone if they be
neglected—else I would not flinch for the stoutest he that wears
a sword. (*Looks big.*)

DOWNRIGHT. What say you, Capitan Whiff? (*Whiff almost drunk.*)

WHIFF. I am trying, Colonel, what mettle I'm made on. I think I   75
am valiant, I suppose I have courage, but I confess, 'tis a little of
the d[evil's] breed, but a little inspiration from the bottle, and
the leave of my Nancy, may do wonders.

(*Enter Seaman in haste.*)

SEAMAN. An't please your Honours, Frightall's officers have seized
all the ships in the river, and rid now round the shore, and had   80
by this time secured the sandy beach, and landed men to fire
the town, but that they are high in drink aboard the ship called
Good Subject; the master of her sent me to let your Honours

---

1 *Speaks big* Variations of this stage direction throughout the play are meant to indicate an
   expression of exaggerated emotion.
2 *to cock ... and bluff* To strut about like a rooster looking for a fight.

know that a few men sent to his assistance will surprise them
85 and retake the ships.

WELLMAN. Now, gentlemen, here's a brave occasion for emulation.
Why writ not the master?

DULLMAN. Aye, had he writ, I had soon been amongst them, i'faith;
but this is some plot to betray us.

90 SEAMAN. Keep me here and kill me if it be not true.

DOWNRIGHT. He says well. There's a brigantine and a shallop[1] ready.
I'll embark immediately.

FRIENDLY. No sir, your presence here is more necessary. Let me have
the honour of this expedition.

95 HAZARD. I'll go your volunteer, Charles.

WELLMAN. Who else offers to go?

WHIMSEY. A mere trick to kidnap us by Bacon. If the Capitan had
writ—

TIMOROUS. Aye, aye, if he had writ—

100 WELLMAN. I see you're all base cowards and here cashier[2] ye from all
commands and offices.

WHIMSEY. Look ye, Colonel, you may do what you please, but you
lose one of the best dressed officers in your whole camp, sir—

TIMOROUS. And in me, such a head-piece.[3]

105 WHIFF. I'll say nothing, but let the state want me.

DULLMAN. For my part, I am weary of weighty affairs.

(*In this while, Wellman, Downright, Friendly, and Hazard talk.*)

WELLMAN. Command what men you please, but expedition makes
you half a conqueror.

(*Exit Friendly and Hazard.*)

(*Enter another Seaman with a letter, gives it to Downright, he and
Wellman read it.*)

---

1   *a brigantine and a shallop*   Different kinds of small boats.
2   *cashier*   Dismiss.
3   *head-piece*   Clever person.

DOWNRIGHT. Look ye now, gentlemen, the master has writ.
DULLMAN. Has he? He might have writ sooner, while I was in 110
command. If he had—
WHIMSEY. Aye, Major—if he had—but let them miss us—
WELLMAN. Colonel, haste with your men and reinforce the beach,
while I follow with the horse. Mr. Dunce, pray let that Procla-
mation be read concerning Bacon to the soldiers. 115
DUNCE. It shall be done, sir.

(*Exit Downright and Wellman.*)

(*The scene opens and discovers a body of soldiers.*)[1]

Gentlemen, how simply you look now.
TIMOROUS. Why, Mr. Parson, I have a scruple of conscience upon
me. I am considering whether it be lawful to kill, though it be
in war. I have a great aversion to it, and hope it proceeds from 120
religion.
WHIFF. I remember the fit took you just so, when the Dutch
besieged us, for you could not then be persuaded to strike a
stroke.
TIMOROUS. Aye, that was because they were Protestants as we are. 125
But gadzoors, had they been Dutch papists[2] I had mauled them!
But conscience ...
WHIMSEY. I have been Justice of Peace these six years and never had
a conscience in my life.
TIMOROUS. Nor I neither, but in this damned thing of fighting. 130
DUNCE. (*To the soldiers.*) Gentlemen, I am commanded to read the
Declaration of the Honourable Council to you.
ALL. Hum hum hum—
BOOZER. Silence! Silence!
DUNCE. "By an Order of Council dated May the 10th, 1670: To 135
all Gentlemen Soldiers, Merchants, Planters, and whom else it
may concern. Whereas Bacon, contrary to law and equity, has,

---

1   *The scene ... soldiers*   The stage direction here seems to indicate a new scene, though the
first edition only indicates two scenes in Act 3.
2   *papists*   Pejorative term for Catholics.

140 to satisfy his own ambition, taken up arms, with a pretense to fight the Indians, but indeed to molest and enslave the whole colony, and to take away their liberties and properties; this is to declare, that whomever shall bring this traitor dead or alive to the Council shall have three hundred pounds reward. And so God save the King."

ALL. A Council! A Council! Hah!

(*Halloo. Enter a Soldier hastily.*)

145 SOLDIER. Stand to your arms, gentlemen, stand to your arms. Bacon is marching this way!

DUNCE. Hah! What numbers has he?

SOLDIER. About a hundred horse. In his march he has surprised Colonel Downright and taken him prisoner.

150 ALL. Let's fall on Bacon! Let's fall on Bacon! Hey! (*Halloo.*)

BOOZER. We'll hear him speak first and see what he can say for himself.

ALL. Aye! Aye! We'll hear Bacon speak! (*Dunce pleads with them.*)

TIMOROUS. Well, Major, I have found a stratagem shall make us
155 four the greatest men in the colony! We'll surrender ourselves to Bacon and say we disbanded on purpose!

DULLMAN. Good—

WHIFF. Why, I had no other design in the world in refusing to fight.

WHIMSEY. Nor I. D'ye think I would have excused it with the fear
160 of disordering my cravat string else?

DUNCE. Why, gentlemen, he designs to fire James-Town, murder you all, and then lie with your wives, and will you slip this opportunity of seizing him?

BOOZER. Here's a termagant rogue, neighbours! We'll hang the dog.

165 ALL. Aye! Hang Bacon! Hang Bacon!

(*Enter Bacon and Fearless, some soldiers leading in Downright, bound; Bacon stands and stares awhile on the regiments, who are silent all.*)

BACON. Well, gentlemen—in order to your fine Declaration you see I come to render myself.

DUNCE. How came he to know of our Declaration?

WHIMSEY. Rogues, rogues among ourselves that inform!

BACON. What, are ye silent all? Not a man lift his hand in obedience 170
to the council to murder this traitor that has exposed his life so
often for you? Ha, what? Not for three hundred pounds! You see
I've left my troops behind and come all wearied with the toils of
war, worn out by summers' heats and winters' colds, marched
tedious days and nights through bogs and fens as dangerous as 175
your clamors and as faithless—what though 'twas to preserve
you all in safety—no matter, you should obey the grateful
council and kill this honest man that has defended you.

ALL. Hum, hum, hum.

WHIFF. The general speaks like a Gorgon.[1] 180

TIMOROUS. Like a cherubim, man.

BACON. All silent yet? Where's that mighty courage that cried so
loud but now, "A Council, a Council"? Where's your resolution?
Cannot three hundred pounds excite your valour to seize that
Bacon who has bled for you? 185

ALL. A Bacon, a Bacon, a Bacon— (*Halloo.*)

DOWNRIGHT. O villainous cowards! Oh, the faithless multitudes!

BACON. What say you, parson? You have a forward zeal?

DUNCE. I wish my coat,[2] sir, did not hinder me from acting as
becomes my zeal and duty. 190

WHIMSEY. A plaguey, rugged dog, that parson.

BACON. Fearless, seize me that canting knave from out the herd, and
next those honourable officers. (*Points to Dullman, Whimsey,
Whiff, and Timorous.*)

(*Fearless seizes them, gives them to the soldiers, and takes the proclamation from Dunce and shows Bacon; they read it.*)

DULLMAN. Seize us, sir, you shall not need. We laid down our com- 195
missions on purpose to come over to your Honour.

---

1   *Gorgon*   In Greek mythology, the Gorgons were three hideous sisters who could turn all
who looked on them to stone. The comparison suggests that Bacon's speech has paralyzed
the crowd.

2   *coat*   I.e., the garments indicating his profession as a parson.

WHIFF. We ever loved and honoured your Honour.

TIMOROUS. (*Aside*.) So entirely, sir, that I wish I were safe in James-Town for your sake, and your Honour were hanged.

200 BACON. This fine piece is of your penning, parson, though it be countenanced by the council's names. Oh, ingratitude! Burn, burn the treacherous town! Fire it immediately!

WHIMSEY. We'll obey you, sir.

WHIFF. Aye, aye, we'll make a bonfire on't, and drink your Honour's

205 health round about it. (*They offer to go.*)

BACON. Yet hold; my revenge shall be more merciful. I ordered that all the women of rank shall be seized and brought to my camp. I'll make their husbands pay their ransoms dearly. They'd rather have their hearts bleed than their purses.

210 FEARLESS. Dear General, let me have the seizing of Colonel Downright's daughter. I would fain be plundering for a trifle called a maidenhead.

BACON. On pain of death treat them all with respect. Assure them of the safety of their honour. Now, all that will follow me shall

215 find a welcome. Those that will not may depart in peace.

ALL. Hey, a general, a general, a general.

(*Some soldiers go off, some go to the side of Bacon.*)

(*Enter Daring and soldiers with Chrisante, Surelove, Mrs. Whimsey and Mrs. Whiff, and several other women.*)

BACON. Successful Daring, welcome. What prizes have ye?

DARING. The fairest in the world, sir. I am not for common plunder.

DOWNRIGHT. Hah! My daughter and my kinswoman!

220 BACON. 'Tis not with women, sir, nor honest men like you that I intend to combat. Not their own parents shall be more indulgent, nor better safeguard to their honours, sir. But 'tis to save the expense of blood I seize on their most valued prizes.

DOWNRIGHT. But sir, I know your wild lieutenant-general has long

225 loved my Chrisante, and perhaps, will take this time to force her to consent.

DARING. I own I have a passion for Chrisante, yet by my general's life—or her fair self—what now I act is on the score of war. I scorn to force the maid I do adore.

BACON. Believe me, ladies, you shall have honourable treatment here. 230

CHRISANTE. We do not doubt it, sir, either from you or Daring. If he love me, that will secure my honour, or if he do not, he's too brave to injure me.

DARING. I thank you for your opinion of me, madam. 235

CHRISANTE. But sir, 'tis for my father I plead. To see his reverend hands in servile chains, and then perhaps if stubborn to your will, his head must fall a victim to your anger.

DOWNRIGHT. No, my good, pious girl, I cannot fear ignoble usage from the general, and if thy beauty can preserve thy fame,[1] I 240 shall not mourn in my captivity.

BACON. I'll never deceive your kind opinion of me, ladies. I hope you're all of that opinion too.

SURELOVE. If seizing us, sir, can advance your honour, or be of any use considerable to you, I shall be proud of such a slavery. 245

MRS. WHIMSEY. I hope, sir, we shan't be ravished in your camp.

DARING. Fie, Mrs. Whimsey. Do soldiers use to ravish?

MRS. WHIFF. Ravish? Marry[2] I fear 'em not. I'd have them know I scorn to be ravished by any man!

FEARLESS. Aye, on my conscience, Mrs. Whiff, you are too good 250 natured.

DARING. Madam, I hope you'll give me leave to name love to you, and try all submissive ways to win your heart?

CHRISANTE. Do your worst, sir. I give you leave—if you assail me only with your tongue. 255

DARING. That's generous and brave, and I'll requite it.

(*Enter* [*a*] *soldier in haste.*)

SOLDIER. The truce being ended, sir, the Indians grow so insolent as to attack us even in our camp, and have killed several of our men.

---

1 *fame* I.e., reputation, honor; virginity.
2 *Marry* Indeed.

260   BACON. 'Tis time to check their boldness. Daring, haste, draw up
      our men in order to give 'em battle. I rather had expected their
      submission.
      The country now may see what they're to fear
      Since we that are in arms are not secure.

      (*Exeunt leading the ladies.*)

ACT 4, SCENE I

(*A temple, with an Indian god placed upon it, priests and priestesses
attending; enter Indian King on one side attended by Indian men,
the Queen enters on the other side with women, all bow to the idol,
and divide on each side of the stage, then the music playing louder, the
priests and priestesses dance about the idol, with ridiculous postures
and crying (as for incantations). Thrice repeated, "Agah Yerkin, Agah
Boah, Sulen Tawarapah, Sulen Tawarapah."*[1] *After this, soft music
plays again, then they sing something fine, after which the priests lead
the King to the altar, and the priestess, the Queen; they take off little
crowns from their heads and offer them at the altar.*)

KING. Invoke the god of our Quiocto[2] to declare what the event
      shall be of this our last war against the English General. (*Soft
      music ceases.*)

(*The music changes to confused tunes, to which the priest and priestess
dance antically, singing between the same incantation as before, and
then dance again, and so invoke again alternately; which dance ended
a voice behind the altar cries, while soft music plays:*)

    The English general shall be,
5   A captive to his enemy;
    And you from all your toils be freed,
    When by your hand the foe shall bleed;

---

1   *Agah Yerkin ... Sulen Tawarapah* These words do not reflect any Algonquian or other
    languages spoken by Indigenous peoples in the region.
2   *Quiocto* Behn's source for this deity name is unclear; she may have invented it.

And ere the sun's swift course be run,
This mighty conquest shall be won.

KING. I thank the gods for taking care of us. Prepare a new sacrifice   10
against the evening. When I return a conqueror, I will myself
perform the office of a priest.

QUEEN. Oh sir, I fear you'll fall a victim first!

KING. What means Semernia? Why are thy looks so pale?

QUEEN. Alas! The oracles have double meanings. Their sense is   15
doubtful and their words enigmas. I fear, sir, I could make a
truer interpretation—

KING. How Semernia? By all thy love, I charge thee as you respect
my life to let me know your thoughts.

QUEEN. Last night I dreamed a lion fell with hunger, despite your   20
guards slew you, and bore you hence!

KING. This is thy sex's fear and no interpretation of the oracle.

QUEEN. I could convince you further.

KING. Hast thou a secret thou canst keep from me? Thy soul a
thought that I must be stranger to? This is not like the justice of   25
Semernia; come, unriddle me the oracle.

QUEEN. The English general shall be a captive to his enemy; he is so
sir, already, to my beauty. He says he languishes for love of me.

KING. Hah! The general is my rival! But go on.

QUEEN. And you from all your war be freed. Oh let me not explain   30
that final line for fear it mean you shall be freed by death.

KING. What, when by my hand the foe shall bleed? Away—it
cannot be.

QUEEN. No doubt, my lord, you'll bravely sell your life and deal
some wounds where you'll receive so many.   35

KING. 'Tis love, Semernia, makes thee dream. While waking, I'll
trust the gods and am resolved for battle.

(*Enter an Indian.*)

INDIAN. Haste, haste great sir to arms! Bacon with all his forces is
prepared and both the armies ready to engage.

KING. Haste to my general. Bid him charge them instantly. I'll bring   40 up the supplies of stout Teroomians,[1] those so well skilled in the envenomed arrow.

(*Exit Indian.*)

Semernia, words but poorly do express the griefs of parting lovers—'tis with dying eyes, and a heart trembling—thus—(*Puts her hand on his heart.*)—they take a heavy leave. One parting kiss, and one love-pressing sigh, and then farewell. But not a long farewell. I shall return victorious to thy arms. Commend me to the gods and still remember me.

(*Exit King.*)

QUEEN. Alas! What pity 'tis I saw the general before my fate had given me to the king. But now, like those that change their gods, my faithless mind 'twixt two opinions wavers. While to the gods my monarch I commend, my wandering thoughts in pity of the general makes that zeal cold, declined—ineffectual; if for the general I implore the deities, methinks my prayers should not ascend the skies since honour tells me 'tis an impious zeal.
Which way soever my devotions move,
I am too wretched to be heard above.

(*Goes in; all exeunt.*)

ACT 4, SCENE 2

(*Shows a field of tents, seen at some distance through the trees of a wood; drums, trumpets, and the noise of battle with hallooing. The Indians are seen with battle-axes to retreat fighting from the English and all go off, when they re-enter immediately beating back the English, the Indian King at the head of his men, with bows and arrows; Daring being at the head of the English. They fight off; the noise continues less loud as more at distance.*)

---

1   *Teroomians*   Possibly another invention of Behn's.

(*Enter Bacon with his sword drawn, meets Fearless with his sword drawn.*)

FEARLESS. Haste, haste, sir, to the entrance of the wood! Daring's engaged past hope of a retreat, venturing too far pursuing the foe. The King in ambush with his poisoned archers fell on and now we're dangerously distressed.
BACON. Daring is brave, but he's too rash. Come on and follow me   5
to his assistance. (*Go out.*)

(*A hallooing within, the fight renews; enter the Indians beaten back by Daring and Fearless; they fight off, the noise of fighting continues a while, this still behind the wood. Enter Indians flying over the stage, pursued by the King.*)

KING. Turn, turn, ye fugitive slaves, and face the enemy! Oh villains, cowards, deaf to all command. By heaven I had my rival in my view and aimed at nothing but my conquering him. Now, like a coward I must fly with cowards or like a desperate madman fall,   10
thus singly, midst the numbers. (*Follows the Indians.*)

(*Enter Bacon enraged, with his sword drawn, Fearless and Daring following him.*)

BACON. Where is the King? Oh ye perfidious slaves, how have you hid [him] from my just revenge? Search all the breaks, the furzes, and the trees, and let him not escape on pain of death!
DARING. We cannot do wonders, sir.   15
BACON. But you can run away—
DARING. Yes, when we see occasion. Yet, should any but my general tell me so—by heaven, he should find I were no starter.[1]
BACON. Forgive me, I'm mad. The King's escaped, hid like a trembling slave in some close ditch where he will sooner starve than   20
fight it out.

---

1 *starter* Deserter.

(Re-enter Indians running over the stage, pursued by the King who shoots them as they fly; some few follow him.)

KING. (*In rage.*) All's lost! The day is lost, and I'm betrayed! Oh slaves, that even wounds can't animate.

BACON. The King!

25 KING. The general here, by all the powers betrayed by my own men.

BACON. Abandoned as thou art I scorn to take thee basely. You shall have a soldier's chance, sir, for your life, since chance so luckily has brought us hither. Without more aids, we will dispute the day. This spot of earth bears both our armies' fates. I'll give you

30 back the victory I have won, and thus begin anew on equal terms.

KING. That's nobly said. The powers have heard my wish! You, sir, first taught me how to use a sword, which heretofore has served me with success. But now, 'tis for Semernia that it draws, a prize

35 more valued than my kingdom, sir.

BACON. Hah! Semernia!

KING. Your blushes do betray your passion for her.

DARING. 'Sdeath, have you fought for this, to expose the victor to the conquered foe?

40 FEARLESS. What, fight a single man—our prize already.

KING. Not so, young man, while I command a dart.

BACON. Fight him, by heaven no reason shall dissuade me, and he that interrupts me is a coward, whatever be my fate. I do command ye to let the King pass freely to his tents.

45 DARING. The devil's in the General.

FEARLESS. 'Sdeath, his romantic humour will undo us.

(They fight and pause.)

KING. You fight as if you meant to outdo me this way, as you have done in generosity.

BACON. You're not behindhand with me, sir, in courtesy. Come,

50 here's to set us even.

(Fight again.)

KING. You bleed apace.

BACON. You've only breathed a vein[1] and given me new health and vigor by it.

(*They fight again, wounds on both sides, the King staggers, Bacon takes him in his arms, the King drops his sword.*)

How do you, sir?

KING. Like one—that's hovering between heaven and earth. I'm   55
mounting—somewhere—upwards—but giddy with my flight—
I know not where.

BACON. Command my surgeons—instantly—make haste! Honour returns and love all bleeding's fled.

(*Exit Fearless.*)

KING. Oh, Semernia, how much more truth had thy divinity than   60
the predictions of the flattering oracles. Commend me to her—I
know you'll—visit—your fair captive, sir, and tell her—oh—but
death prevents the rest. (*Dies.*)

(*Enter Fearless.*)

BACON. He's gone—and how like Caesar[2] I could weep over the
hero I myself destroyed.   65

FEARLESS. I'm glad for your repose. I see him there—t'was a mad,
hot-brained youth, and so he died.

BACON. Come, bear him on your shoulders to my tent, from
whence, with all the solemn state we can, we will convey him to
his own pavilion.   70

(*Enter a soldier.*)

SOLDIER. Some of our troops, pursuing of the enemy even to their

---

1 *breathed a vein*   Reference to the medical practice of bloodletting.
2 *like Caesar*   In Plutarch's account, Caesar wept when presented with the head of his enemy and former political ally Pompey.

temples, which they made their sanctuary, finding the Queen at her devotion there with all her Indian ladies, I'd much ado to stop their violent rage from setting fire to the holy pile.

75 BACON. Hang them immediately that durst attempt it, while I myself fly to rescue her.

(*Goes out. They bear off the King's body, exeunt all.*)

(*Enter Whimsey, pulling in Whiff, with a halter about his neck.*)

WHIMSEY. Nay, I'm resolved to keep thee here till his Honour the General comes—what—to call him traitor and run away after he had so generously given us our freedom and listed us cadets
80 for the next command that fell in his army. I'm resolved to hang thee—

WHIFF. Wilt thou betray and 'peach[1] thy friend? Thy friend that kept thee company all the while thou wert a prisoner—drinking at my own charge—

85 WHIMSEY. No matter for that. I scorn ingratitude and therefore will hang thee—but as for drinking with me, I scorn to be behind-hand with thee in civility, and therefore, here's to thee. (*Takes a bottle of brandy out of his pocket, drinks.*)

WHIFF. I can't drink.

90 WHIMSEY. A certain sign thou would be hanged.

WHIFF. (*Weeps.*) You used to be on my side when a Justice, let the cause be how it would.

WHIMSEY. Aye, when I was a Justice I never minded honesty, but now, I'll be true to my General, and hang thee to be a great man.

95 WHIFF. If I might but have a fair trial for my life—

WHIMSEY. A fair trial? Come, I'll be thy judge, and if thou canst clear thyself by law, I'll acquit thee. Sirrah, sirrah, what canst thou say for thyself for calling his Honour rebel? (*Sits on a drumhead.*)

100 WHIFF. 'Twas when I was drunk, an't like your Honour.

WHIMSEY. That's no plea, for if you kill a man when you are sober you must be hanged when you are drunk. Hast thou anything

---

1 *'peach* Impeach.

else to say for thyself why sentence may not pass upon thee?

WHIFF. I desire the benefit of the clergy.[1]

WHIMSEY. The clergy! I never knew anybody that ever did benefit by   105
them. Why, thou canst not read a word.

WHIFF. Transportation, then.

WHIMSEY. It shall be to England then. But hold—who's this?

(*Dullman creeping from a bush.*)

DULLMAN. So the danger's over, I may venture out. A pox on't, I
would not be in this fear again to be Lord Chief Justice of our   110
court!

(*Enter Timorous with battle-axe, bow and arrows, and feathers on his
head.*)

Why, how now Cornet. What, in dreadful equipage?[2] Your
battle-axe bloody, with bow and arrows?

TIMOROUS. I'm in the posture of the times, Major. I could not be
idle where so much action was! I'm going to present myself to   115
the General with these trophies of my victory here.

DULLMAN. Victory? What victory? Did not [I] see thee creeping out
of yonder bush where thou wert hid all the fight, stumble on a
dead Indian, and take away his arms?

TIMOROUS. Why, didst thou see me?   120

DULLMAN. See thee? Aye, and what a fright thou wert in till thou
wert sure he was dead.

TIMOROUS. Well, well, that's all one. Gadzoors, if every man that
passed for valiant in a battle were to give an account how he
gained his reputation, the world would be but thinly stocked   125
with heroes. I'll say he was a great war captain, and that I killed
him hand to hand, and who can disprove me?

DULLMAN. Disprove thee? Why, that pale face of thine that has so
much coward in it.

---

1   *benefit of the clergy*   Legal provision under which members of the clergy could avoid
    prosecution under the secular court and be tried instead in an ecclesiastical court.
2   *dreadful equipage*   Military attire or equipment.

130 TIMOROUS. Pshaw, that's with loss of blood! Hah, I am overheard I doubt[1]—who's yonder? (*Sees Whimsey and Whiff.*) How, brother Whiff in a hempen cravat-string?[2]

WHIMSEY. He called the General traitor and was running away, and I'm resolved to peach.

135 DULLMAN. Hum—and one witness will stand good in law, in case of treason.

TIMOROUS. Gadzoors, in case of treason he'll be hanged if it be proved against him, were there ne'er a witness at all; but he must [be] tried by a council of war, man—come, come, let's disarm him.

(*They take away him arms, and pull a bottle of brandy out of his pocket.*)

140 WHIFF. What, I hope you will not take away my brandy, gentlemen, my last comfort.

TIMOROUS. Gadzoors, it's come in good time! Well, drink it off, here Major. (*Drinks; Whiff takes him aside.*)

WHIFF. Hark ye, Cornet—you are my good friend. Get this matter
145 made up before it come to the General.

TIMOROUS. But this is treason, neighbour.

WHIFF. If I hang, I will declare upon the ladder how you killed your war Captain.

TIMOROUS. Come, brother Whimsey. We have been all friends and
150 loving magistrates together. Let's drink about and think no more of this business.

DULLMAN. Aye, aye, if every sober man in the nation should be called to account of the treason he speaks in his drink, the Lord have mercy upon us all! Put it up and let us like loving brothers
155 take an honest resolution to run away together, for this same Frightall minds nothing but fighting.

WHIMSEY. I'm content, provided we go all to the council and tell them (to make our peace) we went in in obedience to the Proclamation to kill Bacon, but the traitor was so strongly guarded
160 we could not effect it. But mum, who's here?

---

1 *doubt* Suspect.

2 *hempen cravat-string* Timorous compares the hempen rope around Whiff's neck to a "cravat" or necktie.

(*To them, enter Ranter and Jenny, as Man and Footman.*)

RANTER. Hah, our four Reverent Justices. I hope the blockheads
will not know me. Gentlemen, can you direct me to Lieutenant
General Daring's tents?

WHIFF. Hum, who the devil's this? That's he that you see coming
this way. 'Sdeath, yonder's Daring. Let's slip away before he   165
advances.

(*Exeunt all but Ranter and Jenny.*)

JENNY. I am scared with those dead bodies we have passed over. For
God's sake, madam, let me know your design in coming.

RANTER. Why? Now I'll tell thee—my damned fellow Daring who
has my heart and soul—loves Chrisante, has stolen her, and   170
carried her away to his tents. She hates him, while I am dying
for him.

JENNY. Dying, madam! I never saw you melancholy.

RANTER. Pox on't, no; why should I sigh and whine, and make
myself an ass, and him conceited, no, instead of snivelling I'm   175
resolved—

JENNY. What, madam?

RANTER. Gad, to beat the rascal and bring off Chrisante.

JENNY. Beat him, madam? What, a woman beat a lieutenant
general?   180

RANTER. Hang 'em. They get a name in war from command, not
courage. How know I but I may fight? Gad, I have known a
fellow kicked from one end of the town to the other believing
himself a coward, at last forced to fight, found he could, got
a reputation and bullied all he met with, and got a name, and   185
with a great commission.

JENNY. But if he should kill you, madam?

RANTER. I'll take care to make it as comical a duel as the best of
them. As much in love as I am, I do not intend to die its martyr.

(*Enter Daring and Fearless.*)

FEARLESS. Have you seen Chrisante since the fight?   190

DARING. Yes, but she is still the same. As nice[1] and coy as Fortune when she's courted by the wretched. Yet she denies me so obligingly she keeps my love still in its humble calm.

RANTER. (*Sullenly.*) Can you direct me, sir, to one Daring's tent?

195 DARING. One Daring? He has another epithet to his name?

RANTER. What's that, rascal or coward?

DARING. Hah! Which of thy stars, young man, has sent thee hither to find that certain fate they have decreed?

RANTER. I know not what my stars have decreed, but I shall be glad
200 if they ordained me to fight with Daring. By thy concern thou shouldst be he?

DARING. I am. Prithee, who art thou?

RANTER. Thy rival, though newly arrived from England, and came to marry fair Chrisante, whom thou hast ravished, for whom I
205 hear another lady dies.

DARING. Dies for me?

RANTER. Therefore resign her fairly—or fight me fairly—

DARING. Come on, sir—but hold—before I kill thee, prithee inform me who this dying lady is?

210 RANTER. Sir, I owe ye no courtesy and therefore will do you none by telling you. Come sir, for Chrisante, draw. (*They offer to fight. Fearless steps in.*)

FEARLESS. Hold! What mad frolic's this? (*To Ranter.*) Sir, you fight for one you never saw. (*To Daring.*) And you for one that loves
215 you not.

DARING. Perhaps she'll love him a little.

RANTER. Gad, put it to the trial, if you dare. If thou be'st generous bring me to her, and whom she does neglect shall give the other place.

220 DARING. That's fair. Put up thy sword. I'll bring thee to her instantly.

(*Exeunt.*)

---

1   *nice*   Fastidious; here with the implication of sexual purity.

ACT 4, SCENE 3

(*A tent.*)

(*Enter Chrisante and Surelove.*)

CHRISANTE. I am not so much afflicted for my confinement as I am
that I cannot hear of Friendly.
SURELOVE. Art not persecuted with Daring?
CHRISANTE. Not at all. Though he tells me daily of his passion, I
rally him, and give him neither hope nor despair.—He's here.   5

(*Enter Daring, Fearless, Ranter, and Jenny.*)

DARING. Madam, the complaisance I show in bringing you my rival
will let you see how glad I am to oblige you every way.
RANTER. I hope the danger I have exposed myself to for the honour
of kissing your hand, madam, will render me something accept-
able. Here are my credentials. (*Gives her a letter.*)   10
CHRISANTE. (*Reads.*) Dear Creature, I have taken this habit to free
you from an impertinent lover and to secure the damned rogue
Daring to myself. Receive me as sent by Colonel Surelove from
England to marry you—favour me—no more—your Ranter.
(*Aside.*) Hah, Ranter? [*To Ranter.*] Sir, you have too good a   15
character from my cousin Colonel Surelove not to receive my
welcome. (*Gives Surelove the letter.*)
RANTER. Stand by, General. (*Pushes away Daring and looks big, and
takes Chrisante by the hand and kisses it.*)
DARING. 'Sdeath, sir, there's room—enough—at first sight so kind?   20
Oh youth—youth and impudence, what temptations are you to
a villainous woman?
CHRISANTE. I confess, sir, we women do not love these rough fight-
ing fellows. They're always scaring us with one broil or other.
DARING. Much good may [it] do you with your tame coxcomb.   25
RANTER. Well, sir, then will you yield the prize?
DARING. Aye, gad, were she an angel that can prefer such a callow
fop as thou before a man. Take her and domineer.

(*They all laugh.*)

—'Sdeath, am I grown ridiculous.

30 FEARLESS. Why, hast thou not found the jest? By heaven, 'tis Ranter!
'Tis she that loves you. (*Aside.*) Carry on the humour. Faith, sir,
if I were you, I would devote myself to Madam Ranter.

CHRISANTE. Aye, she's the fittest wife for you. She'll fit your
humour.

35 DARING. Ranter? Gad, I'd sooner marry a she-bear, unless for a
penance for some horrid sin. We should be eternally challenging
one another to the field, and ten to one she beats me there. Or if
I should escape there, she would kill me with drinking!

RANTER. Here's a rogue. Does your country abound with such
40 ladies?

DARING. The Lord forbid. Half a dozen would ruin the land,
debauch all the men, and scandalize all the women!

FEARLESS. No matter, she's rich.

DARING. Aye, that will make her insolent.

45 FEARLESS. Nay, she's generous too.

DARING. Yes, when she's drunk, and then she'll lavish all.

RANTER. A pox on him. How he vexes me.

DARING. Then such a tongue—she'll rail and smoke till she choke
again, then six gallons of punch hardly recovers her, and never
50 but then is she good natured.

RANTER. I must lay him on.[1]

DARING. There's not a blockhead in the country that has not—

RANTER. What?

DARING. —been drunk with her.

55 RANTER. (*In a huff.*) I thought you had meant something else, sir.

DARING. Nay, as for that, I suppose there's no great difficulty.

RANTER. 'Sdeath, sir, you lie, and you're a son of a whore. (*Draws
and fences with him, and he runs back round the stage.*)

DARING. Hold, hold virago! Dear Widow hold, and give me thy
60 hand.

RANTER. Widow!

DARING. 'Sdeath, I knew thee by instinct Widow, though I seemed

---

1 *lay him on* Beat him.

not to do so in revenge of the trick you put on me in telling me
a lady died for me.

RANTER. Why, such a one there is, perhaps she may dwindle forty   65
or fifty years—or so—but will never be her own woman again,
that's certain.

SURELOVE. This we are all ready to testify. We know her.

CHRISANTE. Upon my life, 'tis true.

DARING. Widow, I have a shrewd suspicion that you yourself may   70
be this dying lady.

RANTER. Why so, coxcomb?

DARING. Because you took such pains to put yourself into my
hands.

RANTER. Gad, if your heart were but half so true as your guess, we   75
should conclude a peace before Bacon and the council will. (*To
Chrisante*.) Besides this thing whines for Friendly and there's no
hopes.

DARING. Give me thy hand, Widow. I am thine—and so entirely,
I will never—be drunk out of thy company! Dunce is in my   80
tent—prithee, let's in, and bind the bargain.

RANTER. Nay, faith, let's see the war's at an end first.

DARING. Nay, prithee, take me in the humour, while thy breeches
are on—for I never liked thee half so well in petticoats.

RANTER. Lead on, General. You give me good encouragement to   85
wear them!

(*Exeunt.*)

ACT 5, SCENE I

(*The savannah in sight of the camp; the moon rises.*)

(*Enter Friendly, Hazard, Boozer, and a party of men.*)

FRIENDLY. We are now in the sight of the tents.

BOOZER. Is not this a rash attempt, gentlemen, with so small force
to set upon Bacon's whole army?

HAZARD. Oh, they are drunk with victory and wine. There will be
naught but revelling tonight.   5

FRIENDLY. Would we could learn in what quarter the ladies are lodged, for we have no other business but to release them. But hark? Who comes here?

BOOZER. Some scouts, I fear, from the enemy.

(*Enter Dullman, Timorous, Whimsey, and Whiff, creeping as in the dark.*)

10   FRIENDLY. Let's shelter ourselves behind yonder trees lest we be surprised.

TIMOROUS. Would I were well at home—gadzoors—if e'er you catch me a cadeeing[1] again, I'll be content to be set in the forefront of the battle for hawks' meat.

15   WHIMSEY. Thou art afraid of every bush.

TIMOROUS. Aye, and good reason too. Gadzoors, there may be rogues hid—prithee, Major, do thou advance.

DULLMAN. No, no, go on. No matter of ceremony in these cases of running away.

(*They advance.*)

20   FRIENDLY. They approach directly to us. We cannot escape them. Their numbers are not great—let us advance.

(*They come up to them.*)

TIMOROUS. Oh! I am annihilated.

WHIFF. Some of Frightall's scouts. We are lost men!

(*They push each other foremost.*)

FRIENDLY. Who goes there?

25   WHIMSEY. Oh, they'll give us no quarter. 'Twas long of you, Cornet, that we ran away from our colours.

TIMOROUS. Me? 'Twas the Major's ambition here to make himself a great man with the council again.

---

1   *a cadeeing*   Pretending to be a cadet.

DULLMAN. Pox on this ambition. It has been the ruin of many a
gallant fellow.   30
WHIFF. If I get home again, the height of mine shall be to top
tobacco. Would I'd some brandy.
TIMOROUS. Gadzoors, would we had! 'Tis the best armour against
fear. Hum—I hear nobody now. Prithee, advance a little.
WHIMSEY. What, before a horse officer?   35
FRIENDLY. Stand on your lives—
TIMOROUS. Oh, 'tis impossible. I'm dead already.
FRIENDLY. What are ye? Speak or I'll shoot!
WHIMSEY. Friends to thee—who the devil are we friends to?
TIMOROUS. E'en who you please, gadzoors.   40
FRIENDLY. Hah—gadzoors—who's there? Timorous?
TIMOROUS. Hum—I know no such scoundrel. (*Gets behind.*)
DULLMAN. Hah—that's Friendly's voice.
FRIENDLY. Right—thine's that of Dullman. Who's with you?
DULLMAN. Only Timorous, Whimsey, and Whiff, all valiantly   45
running away from the arch rebel that took us prisoners.
HAZARD. Can you inform us where the ladies are lodged?
DULLMAN. In the hither quarter in Daring's tents. You'll know
them by lanterns on every corner—there was never better time
to surprise them—for this day Daring's married, and there's   50
nothing but dancing and drinking.
HAZARD. Married? To whom?
DULLMAN. That I ne'er inquired.
FRIENDLY. 'Tis to Chrisante, friend, and the reward of my attempt is
lost. Oh, I am mad, I'll fight away my life and my despair shall   55
yet do greater wonders than even my love could animate me to.
Let's part our men and beset his tents on both sides.

(*Friendly goes out with a party.*)

HAZARD. Come gentlemen, let's on—
WHIFF. On, sir? We on, sir?
HAZARD. Aye, you on, sir—to redeem the ladies.   60
WHIFF. Oh, sir, I am going home for money to redeem my Nancy.
WHIMSEY. So am I, sir.
TIMOROUS. I thank my stars I'm a bachelor. Why, what a plague is a
wife!

65 HAZARD. Will you march forward?
  DULLMAN. We have achieved honour enough already in having
    made our campaign here— (*Looking big.*)
  HAZARD. 'Sdeath, but you shall go. Put them in the front and prick
    them on. If they offer to turn back, run them through!
70 TIMOROUS. Oh, horrid!

(*The soldiers prick them on with their swords.*)

  WHIFF. Oh, Nancy, thy dream will yet come to pass.
  HAZARD. Will you advance, sir? (*Pricks Whiff.*)
  WHIFF. Why, so we do, sir. The devil's in these fighting fellows.

(*Exeunt.*)

(*An alarm at a distance.*)

(*Within.*) To arms, to arms, the enemy's upon us.

(*A noise of fighting, after which enters Friendly with his party, retreating and fighting, from Daring and some Soldiers, Ranter fighting like a Fury[1] by his side, he putting her back in vain; they fight out. Re-enter Daring with Friendly all bloody. Several soldiers enter with flambeaux.*)

75 DARING. Now, sir—what injury have I ever done you, that you
    should use this treachery against me?
  FRIENDLY. To take advantage any way in war was never counted
    treachery—and had I murdered thee, I had not paid thee half
    the debt I owe thee.
80 DARING. You bleed too much to hold too long a parley. Come to
    my tent. I'll take charitable care of thee.
  FRIENDLY. I scorn thy courtesy, who against all the laws of honour
    and justice hast ravished innocent ladies!
  DARING. Sir, your upbraiding of my honour shall never make me
85   forfeit it, or esteem you less. Is there a lady here you have a
    passion for?

---

1 *Fury* Female vengeance deity in Greek mythology.

FRIENDLY. Yes, on a nobler score than thou darest own.

DARING. To let you see how you're mistaken, sir, who e'er that lady be whom you affect, I will resign, and give you both your freedoms. 90

FRIENDLY. Why, for this courtesy, which shows thee brave, in the next fight I'll save thy life to quit the obligation.

DARING. I thank you, sir. Come to my tent, and when we've dressed your wounds and yielded up the ladies, I'll give you my passport for your safe conduct back, and tell your friends in the town 95 we'll visit them in the morning.

FRIENDLY. They'll meet you on your way, sir.

DARING. Come, my young soldier. Now thou'st won my soul.

(*An alarm beats; enter at another passage Boozer with all the ladies; they pass over the stage, while Hazard, Downright, beating back a party of soldiers. Dullman, Timorous, Whimsey, and Whiff, pricked on by their party to fight, so that they lay about them like madmen. Bacon, Fearless, and Daring come in, rescue their men, and fight out the other party, some falling dead. Bacon, Fearless, and Daring return tired, with their swords drawn. Enter Soldier running.*)

SOLDIER. Return, sir, where your sword will be more useful! A party of Indians taking advantage of the night have set fire on your 100 tents and borne away the queen.

BACON. Hah—the queen! By heaven, this victory shall cost them dear. Come, let's fly to rescue her! (*Goes out.*)

ACT 5, SCENE 2

(*Scene changes to Wellman's tent. Enter Wellman, Brag, Grubb, and Officers.*)

WELLMAN. I cannot sleep, my impatience is so great to engage this haughty enemy before they have reposed their weary limbs. Is not yon ruddy light the morning's dawn?

BRAG. 'Tis, and please your Honour.

WELLMAN. Is there no news of Friendly yet, and Hazard? 5

BRAG. Not yet. 'Tis thought they left the camp tonight with some design against the enemy.

WELLMAN. What men have they?

BRAG. Only Boozer's party, sir.

10 WELLMAN. I know they are brave and mean to surprise me with some handsome action.

(*Enter Friendly.*)

FRIENDLY. I ask a thousand pardons, sir, for quitting the camp without your leave.

WELLMAN. Your conduct and your courage cannot err. I see thou'st
15 been in action by thy blood.

FRIENDLY. Sir, I'm ashamed to own these slender wounds, since without more, my luck was to be taken while Hazard did alone effect the business of rescuing the ladies.

WELLMAN. How got ye liberty?

20 FRIENDLY. By Daring's generosity, who sends you word he'll visit you this morning.

WELLMAN. We are prepared to meet him.

(*Enter Downright, Hazard, Ladies, Whimsey, Whiff, Dullman, Timorous looking big; Wellman embraces Downright.*)

WELLMAN. My worthy friend, how am I joyed to see you!

DOWNRIGHT. We owe our liberties to these brave youths who can
25 do wonders when they fight for ladies.

TIMOROUS. With our assistance, ladies.

WHIMSEY. For my part, I'll not take it as I have done. Gad, I find when I am damnable angry I can beat both friend and foe.

WHIFF. When I fight for my Nancy here—adsfish,[1] I'm a dragon.

30 MRS. WHIFF. Lord, you need not have been so hasty.

FRIENDLY. Do not upbraid me with your eyes, Chrisante, but let these wounds assure you I endeavoured to serve you, though Hazard had the honour on't.

WELLMAN. But, ladies, we'll not expose you in the camp. A party of
35 our men shall see you safely conducted to Madam Surelove's— 'tis but a little mile from our camp.

---

1 *adsfish* An oath, with "ads" short for "god's."

FRIENDLY. Let me have that honour, sir.

CHRISANTE. No, I conjure you let your wounds be dressed. Obey me if you love me, and Hazard shall conduct us home.

WELLMAN. He had the toil, 'tis fit he have the recompense. 40

WHIFF. He the toil, sir? What? Did we stand for cyphers?

WHIMSEY. The very appearance I made in the front of the battle awed the enemy.

TIMOROUS. Aye, aye, let the enemy say how I mauled them! But gadzoors, I scorn to brag. 45

WELLMAN. Since you've regained your honour so gloriously, I restore you to your commands you lost by your seeming cowardice.

DULLMAN. Valour is not always in humour, sir.

WELLMAN. Come, gentlemen, since they're resolved to engage us, let's set our men in order to receive 'em. 50

(*Exit all but the four Justices.*)

TIMOROUS. Our commissions again! You must be bragging and see what comes on't. I was modest, ye see, and said nothing of my prowess.

WHIFF. What a devil, does the colonel think we are made of iron, continually to beat on the anvil? 55

WHIMSEY. Look gentlemen, here's two evils: If we go, we are dead men; if we stay, we are hanged, and that will disorder my cravat-string. Therefore, the least evil is to go, and set a good face on the matter as I do! (*Goes out singing.*)

ACT 5, SCENE 3

(*A thick wood.*)

(*Enter Queen dressed like an Indian man with a bow in her hand and quiver at her back, Anaria her confidant disguised too, and about a dozen Indians led by Cavaro.*)

QUEEN. I tremble yet; dost think we're safe, Cavaro?

CAVARO. Madam, these woods are intricate and vast, and 'twill be

difficult to find us out—or if they do, this habit[1] will secure you
from the fear of being taken.

5　QUEEN. Dost think if Bacon find us he will not know me? Alas, my
fears and blushes will betray me.

ANARIA. 'Tis certain, madam, if we stay, we perish, for all the wood's
surrounded by the conqueror.

QUEEN. Alas, 'tis better we should perish here than stay to expect
10　the violence of his passion, to which, my heart's too sensibly
inclined.

ANARIA. Why do you not obey its dictates then? Why do you fly the
conqueror?

QUEEN. Not fly? Not fly the murderer of my lord?

15　ANARIA. What world, what resolution can preserve you? And what
he cannot gain by soft submission, force will at last o'ercome.

QUEEN. I wish there were in Nature one excuse either by force or
reason to compel me. For oh, Anaria! I adore this general. Take
from my soul a truth—till now concealed. At twelve years old,
20　at the Pauwmungian[2] court, I saw this conqueror. I saw him
young and gay as new-born Spring, glorious and charming as
the mid-day sun. I watched his looks, listened when he spoke,
and thought him more than mortal.

ANARIA. He has a graceful form.

25　QUEEN. At last, a fatal match concluded was, between my lord and
me. I gave my hand, but oh how far my heart was from consent-
ing. The angry gods are witness.

ANARIA. 'Twas pity.

QUEEN. Twelve tedious moons I passed in silent languishment,
30　honour endeavoring to destroy my love—but all in vain, for still
my pain returned whenever I beheld my conqueror. (*Fiercely*.)
But now, when I consider him as murderer of my lord, I sigh
and wish some other fatal hand had given him his death. But
now there's a necessity I must be brave and overcome my heart.
35　What if I do? Ah, whither shall I fly? I have no Amazonian fire
about me—all my artillery is sighs and tears, the earth my bed,
and heaven my canopy. (*Weeps*.) (*After a noise of fighting*.) Hah!
We are surprised! Oh, whither shall I fly? And yet, methinks

1　*habit*　Clothing; disguise.
2　*Pauwmungian*　Pamunkey.

a certain trembling joy, spite of my soul, spite of my boasted
honour, runs shivering round my heart.   40

(*Enter an Indian.*)

INDIAN. Madam, your out guards are surprised by Bacon, who hews
down all before him and demands the queen with such a voice
and eyes so fierce and angry, he kills us with his looks.
CAVARO. Draw up your poisoned arrows to the head and aim them
at his heart. Sure some will hit.   45
QUEEN. (*Aside.*) Cruel Cavaro! Would 'twere fit for me to contradict
thy justice.
BACON. (*Within.*) The queen, ye slaves, give me the queen and live!

(*He enters furiously beating back some Indians, Cavaro's party going
to shoot, the Queen runs in.*)

QUEEN. Hold, hold! I do command ye!

(*Bacon flies on them as they shoot and miss him, and fights like a
Fury, and wounds the Queen in the disorder; beats them all out.*)

—hold thy commanding hand, and do not kill me, who would   50
not hurt thee to regain my kingdom—

(*He snatches her in his arms; she reels.*)

BACON. Hah! A woman's voice! What art thou? Oh my fears!
QUEEN. Thy hand has been too cruel to a heart whose crime was
only tender thoughts for thee.
BACON. The queen! What is't my sacrilegious hand has done?   55
QUEEN. The noblest office of a gallant friend. Thou'st saved my
honour and hast given me death.
BACON. Is't possible? Ye unregarding gods, is't possible?
QUEEN. Now I may love you without infamy and please my dying
heart by gazing on you.   60
BACON. Oh, I am lost! Forever lost! I find my brain turn with the
wild confusion.

QUEEN. I faint. Oh, lay me gently on the earth.

(*Lays her down.*)

BACON. Who waits? (*Turns in rage to his men.*) Make of the trophies
65   of the war a pile and set it all on fire, that I may leap into con-
suming flames while all my tents are burning round about me.
(*Wildly.*) Oh thou dear prize for which alone I toiled. (*Weeps
and lies down by her.*)

(*Enter Fearless with his sword drawn.*)

FEARLESS. Hah, on the earth. How do you, sir?
70   BACON. What wouldst thou?
FEARLESS. Wellman with all the forces he can gather attacks us even
in our very camp. Assist us, sir, or all is lost.
BACON. Why, prithee let him make the world his prize. I have no
business with the trifle now. It contains nothing that's worth my
75   care since my fair queen is dead, and by my hand.
QUEEN. So charming and obliging is thy moan that I could wish for
life to recompense it. But oh, death falls—all cold—upon my
heart like mildews on blossoms.
FEARLESS. By heaven, sir, this love will ruin all. Rise, rise, and save
80   us yet!
BACON. Leave me. What e'er becomes of me, lose not thy share of
glory. Prithee, leave me.
QUEEN. Alas, I fear thy fate is drawing on and I shall shortly meet
thee in the clouds. Till then, farewell! Even death is pleasing to
85   me, while thus, I find it in my arms— (*Dies.*)
BACON. There ends my race of glory and of life.

(*An alarm at [a] distance—continues a while.*)

Hah—why should I idly whine away my life, since there are
nobler ways to meet with death? Up, up, and face him then.
Hark! There's the soldier's knell and all the joys of life—with
90   thee, I bid farewell.

([*Bacon and Fearless go*] *out.*)

(*The Indians bear off the body of the Queen.*)

(*The alarm continues. Enter Downright, Wellman, and others, swords drawn.*)

WELLMAN. They fight like men possessed. I did not think to have found them so prepared.
DOWNRIGHT. They've good intelligence—but where's the rebel?
WELLMAN. Sure he's not in the fight. Oh that it were my happy chance to meet him that while our men look on, we might   95
dispatch the business of war. Come, let's fall in again now we have taken breath.

(*They go out. Enter Daring and Fearless hastily, with their swords drawn, meet Whimsey, Whiff, with their swords drawn, running away.*)

DARING. (*In anger.*) How now? Whither away?
WHIMSEY. Hah, Daring here. We are pursuing of the enemy, sir. Stop us not in the pursuit of glory! (*Offer[s] to go.*)   100
DARING. Stay. I have not seen you in my ranks today.
WHIFF. Lord, does your Honour take us for starters?
FEARLESS. Yes, sirrah, and believe you are now rubbing off—confess, or I'll run you through.
WHIFF. Oh mercy, sir, mercy! We'll confess.   105
WHIMSEY. What will you confess? We are only going behind yon hedge to untruss a point,[1] that's all.
WHIFF. Aya, your Honours will smell out the truth if you keep us here long.
DARING. Here, carry them prisoners to my tent.   110

(*Exit Soldier with Whimsey and Whiff.*)

---

1 *untruss a point* Unlace or unbutton a garment; the implication is that they are going to relieve themselves.

(*Enter Ranter, without a hat, and sword drawn. Daring angrily goes the other way.* [*Dullman and Timorous are lying on the ground as if dead.*])

RANTER. A pox of all ill luck! How came I to lose Daring in the fight? Hah! Who's here? Dullman and Timorous dead? The rogues are counterfeits. I'll see what moveables they have about them. All's lawful prize in war.

(*Takes their money, watches, and rings; goes out.*)

115 TIMOROUS. What, rob the dead? Why, what will this villainous world come to?

(*Clashing of swords just as they were going to rise.*)

(*Enter Hazard bringing in Ranter.*)

HAZARD. Thou couldst expect no other fate, young man; thy hands are yet too tender for a sword.
RANTER. Thou lookst like a good-natured fellow. Use me civilly and
120 Daring shall ransom me.
HAZARD. Doubt not a generous treatment. (*Goes out.*)
DULLMAN. So, the coast is clear. I desire to remove my quarters to some place of more safety.

(*They rise and go off.*)

(*Enter Wellman and Soldiers hastily.*)

WELLMAN. 'Twas this way Bacon fled. Five hundred pound for him
125 who finds the rebel. (*Goes out.*)

ACT 5, SCENE 4

(*Scene changes to a wood. Enter Bacon and Fearless with their swords drawn, all bloody.*)

BACON. 'Tis just, ye gods! That when you took the prize for which I fought, Fortune and you should all abandon me.

FEARLESS. Oh fly, sir, to some place of safe retreat. For there's no mercy to be hoped if taken. What will you do? I know we are pursued. By heaven, I will not die a shameful death!   5

BACON. Oh, they'll have pity on thy youth and bravery, but I'm above their pardon.

(*A noise is heard.*)

(*Within.*) This way—this way—hay—halloo.

FEARLESS. Alas, sir, we're undone—I'll see which way they take— (*Exits.*)   10

BACON. So near! Nay then to my last shift. (*Undoes the pommel of his sword.*) Come my good poison, like that of Hannibal.[1] Long I have borne a noble remedy for all the ills of life. (*Takes poison.*) I have too long survived my queen and glory—those two bright stars that influenced my life are set to all eternity. (*Lies down.*)   15

(*Enter Fearless, runs to Bacon and looks on his sword.*)

FEARLESS. Hah! What have you done?

BACON. Secured myself from being a public spectacle upon the common theatre of death.

(*Enter Daring and Soldiers.*)

DARING. Victory, victory! They fly, they fly! Where's the victorious general?   20

---

1 *Hannibal* Carthaginian general (247–c. 181 BCE) who killed himself with poison rather than be taken by his Roman enemies.

FEARLESS. Here—taking his last adieu.

DARING. Dying? Then wither all the laurels on my brows, for I shall never triumph more in war. Where are the wounds?

FEARLESS. From his own hand by what he carried here believing we
25   had lost the victory.

BACON. And is the enemy put to flight, my hero? (*Grasps his neck.*)

DARING. All routed horse and foot. I placed an ambush, and while they were pursuing you, my men fell on behind and won the day.

30 BACON. Thou almost makes me wish to live again, if I could live now fair Semernia's dead. But oh—the baneful drug is just and kind and hastens me away. Now while you are victors, make a peace—with the English council—and never let ambition—love—or interest make you forget as I have done—your
35   duty—and allegiance. Farewell—a long farewell— (*Dies embracing their necks.*)

DARING. So fell the Roman Cassius[1] by mistake.

(*Enter Soldiers with Dunce, Timorous, and Dullman.*)

SOLDIER. An't please your Honour, we took these men running away.

40 DARING. Let 'em loose—the wars are at an end. See where the general lies? That great-souled man, no private body e'er contained a nobler. And he that could have conquered all America finds only here his scanty length of earth. Go bear the body to his own pavilion. (*Soldiers go out with the body.*) Though we are
45   conquerors, we submit to treat, and yield upon conditions. You, Mr. Dunce, shall bear our articles to the Council.

DUNCE. With joy, I obey you.

(*Exit Dunce.*)

---

1 *Cassius* After the assassination of Julius Caesar, two battles took place at Phillipi, one between the forces of Brutus and Mark Antony and the other between the forces of Cassius and Octavius Caesar (42 BCE). Cassius killed himself, thinking Brutus had been defeated and that he would fall to Octavius.

TIMOROUS. Good General, let us be put in the agreement.
DARING. You shall be obliged.

(*Exeunt Daring, Dunce, Dullman, and Timorous; as Fearless goes out, a Soldier meets him.*)

SOLDIER. What does your Honour intend to do with Whimsey and   50
Whiff who are condemned by a Council of War?

(*Enter Daring, Dullman, Fearless, and Officers.*)

DARING. You come too late, gentlemen, to be put into the Articles,
nor am I satisfied you're worthy of it.
DULLMAN. Why, did not you, sir, see us lie dead in the field?
DARING. Yes, but I see no wound about you.   55
TIMOROUS. We were stunned with being knocked down! Gadzoors,
a man may be killed with the butt end of a musket as soon as
with the point of a sword!

(*Enter Dunce.*)

DUNCE. The council, sir, wishes you health and happiness, and sends
you these signed by their hands. (*Gives papers.*)   60
DARING. (*Reads.*) "That you shall have a general pardon for yourself
and friends, that you shall have all new commissions, and
Daring to command as general; that you shall have free leave to
inter your dead general in James-Town; and to ratify this, we
will meet you at Madam Surelove's house which stands between   65
the armies, attended only by your officers." The council is noble
and I'll wait upon them.

(*Exit Dunce.*)

Act 5, Scene 5

(A grove near Madam Surelove's; enter Surelove weeping, Wellman, Chrisante, Mrs. Flirt, Ranter [dressed] as before, Downright, Hazard, Friendly, Boozer, Brag.)

WELLMAN. How long, madam, have you heard the news of Colonel Surelove's death?

SURELOVE. By a vessel last night arrived.

WELLMAN. You should not grieve when men so old pay their debt
5 to Nature. You are too fair not to have been reserved for some young lover's arms.

HAZARD. I dare not speak—but give me leave to hope.

SURELOVE. The way to oblige me to it is never more to speak to me of love till I shall think it fit.

(Wellman speaks to Downright.)

10 WELLMAN. Come, you shan't grant it—'tis a hopeful youth.

DOWNRIGHT. You are too much my friend to be denied. Chrisante, do you love Friendly? Nay, do not blush till you have done a fault. Your loving him is none. Here, take her, young man, and with her all my fortune—when I am dead, sirrah, not a groat
15 before unless to buy you baby clouts.[1]

FRIENDLY. He merits not this treasure, sir, can wish for more.

(Enter Daring, Fearless, Dunce, and Officers; they meet Wellman and Downright who embrace them. Dullman and Timorous stand.)

DARING. Can you forgive us, sir, our disobedience?

WELLMAN. Your offering peace while yet you might command it has made such kind impressions on us that now you may com-
20 mand your propositions. Your pardons are all sealed and new commissions.

DARING. I'm not ambitious of that honour, sir, but in obedience will accept your goodness. But sir, I hear I have a young friend taken prisoner by Captain Hazard whom I entreat you'll render me.

---

1   *clouts* Clothes.

HAZARD. Sir—here, I resign him to you. (*Gives him Ranter.*)   25
RANTER. Faith, General, you left me but scurvily in battle.
DARING. That was to see how well you could shift for yourself. Now
  that I find you can bear the brunt of a campaign, you are a fit
  wife for a soldier.
ALL. A woman! Ranter!   30
HAZARD. Faith, madam, I should have given you kinder quarter if I
  had known my happiness.
FLIRT. I have a humble petition to you, sir.
SURELOVE. In which we all join.
FLIRT. An't please you, sir, Mr. Dunce has long made love to me and   35
  on promise of marriage, has— (*Simpers.*)
DOWNRIGHT. What has he, Mrs. Flirt?
FLIRT. Only been a little familiar with my person, sir.
WELLMAN. Do you hear, Parson? You must marry Mrs. Flirt.
DUNCE. How, sir, a man of my coat, sir, marry a brandy-monger?   40
WELLMAN. (*Aside to him.*) Of your calling you mean, a farrier and
  no parson. She'll leave her trade and spark it above all the ladies
  at church. No more! Take her and make her honest.

(*Enter Whimsey and Whiff, stripped.*)

CHRISANTE. Bless me, what have we here?
WHIMSEY. Why, an't like your Honours, we were taken by the   45
  enemy—hah, Daring here and Fearless?
FEARLESS. How now, gentlemen. Were not you two condemned to
  be shot for running from your colours?[1]
DOWNRIGHT. From your colours?
FEARLESS. Yes sir, they were both listed in my regiment.   50
DOWNRIGHT. Then we must hang them for deserting us.
WHIMSEY. So out of the frying pan—you know where, brother—
WHIFF. Aye, he that's born to be hanged[2]—you know the rest, a pox
  of these proverbs.
WELLMAN. I know ye well. You're all rank cowards. But once more,   55
  we forgive ye; your places in the council shall be supplied by

---

1 *colours* Flags of a given regiment.
2 *he that's ... hanged* Common proverb: He that's born to be hanged will never be
   drowned.

these gentlemen of sense and honour. The governor when he comes shall find the country in better hands than he expects to find it.

60 WHIMSEY. A very fair discharge.

WHIFF. I'm glad 'tis no worse. I'll home to my Nancy.

DULLMAN. Have we exposed our lives and fortunes for this?

TIMOROUS. Gadzoors, I never thrived since I was a statesman, left planting, and fell to promising and lying. I'll to my old trade
65 again, bask under the shade of my own tobacco, and drink my punch in peace.

WELLMAN. Come my brave youths, let all our forces meet,
To make this country happy, rich, and great;
Let scanted Europe see that we enjoy
70 Safer repose, and larger worlds than they.

FINIS.

In Context

John Dryden's prologue and epilogue for *The Widow Ranter* (1689)

Many Restoration-era plays were accompanied by verse prologues and epilogues that had been written by someone other than the play's original author. The first edition of *The Widow Ranter* (1690) was published with a prologue and epilogue written by the prominent poet, dramatist, and literary critic John Dryden—but both were originally intended for different publications. The prologue had been written for a play by Thomas Shadwell called *A True Widow* (1678), and the epilogue had appeared years earlier in *Covent-Garden Drollery: A Miscellany of 1672*. Dryden had also, however, written a prologue and epilogue specifically for the 1689 performance of *The Widow Ranter*. These are printed here.

[PROLOGUE]

(Spoken by a woman)

Plays you will have; and to supply your store,
Our poets trade to every foreign shore:
This is the product of Virginian ground,
And to the port of Covent-Garden[1] bound.
Our cargo is, or should at least, be wit: 5
Bless us from you damned pirates of the pit:[2]
And vizard-masks,[3] those dreadful apparitions;

---

1   *Covent-Garden*   London's West End district noted at the time for its taverns, theaters, and brothels.

2   *pirates of the pit*   The metaphor of the play as a ship's cargo is extended here to include its reception. Pirates are a danger both at sea and in London, where they are found in the "pit"—the area in the theater just before the stage.

3   *vizard-masks*   Small masks worn to disguise the face. The term also came to refer to the women who wore them, both fashionable ladies and prostitutes alike.

She-privateers, of venomous conditions,
That clap us oft aboard with French commissions.[1]
10 You sparks,[2] we hope, will wish us happy trading;
For you have ventures in our vessel's lading;
And though you touch at this or t'other nation;
Yet sure Virginia is your dear[3] plantation.
Expect no polished scenes of love should rise
15 From the rude growth of Indian colonies.
Instead of courtship, and a tedious pother,[4]
They only tip the wink at one another;
Nay often the whole nation, pig together.[5]
You civil beaux, when you pursue the game,[6]
20 With manners mince the meaning of—that same:
But every part has there its proper name.
Good Heavens defend me, who am yet unbroken
From living there, where such bug[7] words are spoken:
Yet surely, Sirs, it does good stomachs show,
25 To talk so savourly[8] of what they do.
But were I bound to that broad speaking land,
What e'er they said, I would not understand,
But innocently, with a lady's grace,
Would learn to whisk my fan about my face.
30 However, to secure you, let me swear,
That no such base mundungus[9] stuff is here.
We bring you of the best the soil affords:
Buy it for once, and take it on our words.

---

1   *She-privateers ... commissions*   Privateers were armed ships that could be hired out to aid governments at war. In Dryden's construction, these ships are gendered female and armed with "venomous conditions" commissioned by the French, whom the English often stereotyped as being prone to sexually transmitted diseases. The suggestion is that these "she-privateers" on the waterways will interrupt the trade ships en route to their destinations, and infect those on board with venereal disease. The conceit is furthered by the use of the verb "clap," playing on the term's common usage at the time as slang for gonorrhea.
2   *sparks*   Young men.
3   *dear*   Favorite.
4   *pother*   Ruckus or fuss.
5   *pig together*   Root around in the same sty.
6   *game*   I.e., sexual conquest.
7   *bug*   Proud, haughty.
8   *savourly*   With pleasure.
9   *mundungus*   Bad-smelling (usually with reference to cheap tobacco).

You would not think a country-girl the worse,
If clean and wholesome, though her linen's coarse.   35
Such are our scenes; and I dare boldly say,
You may laugh less at a far better play.
The story's true; the fact not long ago;
The hero of our stage was English too:
And bate[1] him one small frailty of rebelling,   40
As brace as e'er was born at Iniskelling.[2]

[EPILOGUE]

(Spoken by a woman)

By this time you have liked, or damned our plot;
Which though I know, my Epilogue knows not:
For if it could foretell, I should not fail,
In decent wise, to thank you, or to rail.
But he who sent me here, is positive,   5
This farce of government[3] is sure to thrive;
Farce is a food as proper for your lips,
As for green-sickness,[4] crumped tobacco pipes.[5]
Besides, the author's dead,[6] and here you sit,
Like the infernal judges of the pit:[7]   10
Be merciful; for 'tis in you this day,
To save or damn her soul; and that's her play.
She who so well could love's kind passion paint,
We piously believe, must be a saint:
Men are but bunglers, when they would express   15
The sweets of love, the dying tenderness;

---

1   *bate*   Excepting.
2   *Iniskelling*   Refers to Enniskillen, a town in northern Ireland, from which hailed a small
    but fierce army that had defeated a Jacobite force in 1689.
3   *farce of government*   The colonial government depicted in the play.
4   *green-sickness*   An illness (now generally referred to as hypochromic anemia) that appar-
    ently tinged the skin green.
5   *crumped*   Curved;   *tobacco pipes*   Reference to the belief held by some in the seven-
    teenth century that tobacco had medicinal qualities.
6   *the author's dead*   Aphra Behn died in the spring of 1689; *The Widow Ranter* was
    posthumously performed.
7   *pit*   The "pit" of hell, but also the section in the theater just before the stage.

But women, by their own abundance, measure,
And when they write, have deeper sense of pleasure.
Yet though her pen did to the mark arrive,
20 'Twas common praise, to please you, when alive;
But of no other woman you have read,
Except this one, to please you, now she's dead.
'Tis like the fate of bees, whose golden pains,
Themselves extinguished, in their hive remains.
25 Or in plain terms to speak, before we go,
What you young gallants, by experience know,
This is an orphan child; a bouncing boy,
'Tis late to lay him out, or to destroy.
Leave your dog-tricks, to lie and to forswear,
30 Pay you for nursing, and we'll keep him here.

from G.J.,[1] the dedication of *The Widow Ranter* to Madam Welldon (1690)

This letter, which was included as a preface to the 1690 edition of the play, provides a glimpse into Behn's connection with her patrons and her critics. It further details the failure of *The Widow Ranter* in production and offers some theories as to why it was a flop. Those details suggest that there may have been parts of the play that were omitted from the print version.

To the much Honoured Madam Welldon.[2]

Madam,

Knowing Mrs. Behn in her lifetime designed to dedicate some of her

---

1 *G.J.* Identified by Janet Todd as George Jenkins. (See Todd, *The Works of Aphra Behn*, vol. 7 [Columbus: Ohio State University Press, 1992], 287.)

2 *Madam Welldon* The identity of the patroness referred to here as "Madam Welldon" is unknown, though Aaron R. Walden indicates that she was connected to "a prominent royalist family." (See *The Widow Ranter*, ed. Aaron R. Walden [New York: Garland Publishing, 1993], 1).

works to you, you have a natural title and claim to this, and I could not, without being unjust to her memory, but fix your name to it, who have not only a wit above that of most of your sex, but a goodness and affability extremely charming and engaging beyond measure. And perhaps there are few to be found like you that are so eminent for hospitality, and a ready and generous assistance to the distressed and indigent, which are qualities that carry much more of divinity with them than a Puritanical outward zeal for virtue and religion.

Our author, Madam, who was so true a judge of wit, was (no doubt of it) satisfied in the patroness she had pitched upon. If ever she had occasion for a wit and sense like yours, 'tis now, to defend this (one of the last of her works) from the malice of her enemies, and the ill nature of the critics, who have had ingratitude enough not to consider the obligations they had to her when living; but to do those gentlemen justice, 'tis not (altogether) to be imputed to their criticism that the play had not that success which it deserved, and was expected by her friends. The main fault ought to lie on those who had the management of it. Had our author been alive, she would have committed it to the flames rather than have suffered it to have been acted with such omissions as was made, and on which the foundation of the play depended.[1] For example, they thought it fit to leave out a whole scene of the Virginian Court of Judicature, which was a lively resemblance of that country justice, and on which depended a great part of the plot, and wherein were many unusual and very natural jests which would at least have made some sort of people laugh. In another part of the play is omitted the appearance of the ghost of the Indian King, killed by Bacon, and though the like may have been represented in other plays, yet I never heard or found but that the sight was very agreeable to an audience, and very awful. Besides, the apparition of the ghost was necessary, for it was that which struck a terror in the Queen and frightened her from harkening to the love of Bacon, believing it a horrid thing to receive the careless embraces of her husband's murderer. And lastly, many of the parts being false[2] cast, and given to those whose talents and genius suited not our author's intention. These, Madam, are some of the

---

1 *such omissions.... depended* The exact nature of these "omissions" is unclear; the scenes mentioned are not included in the printed text of the play.
2 *false* I.e., poorly.

reasons that this play was unsuccessful, and the best play that was ever writ must prove so if it have the fate to be murdered like this.

However, Madam, I can't but believe you will find an hour's diversion in the reading, and will meet with not only wit, but true comedy (though low), by reason many of the characters are such only as our Newgate[1] afforded, being criminals transported.

This play, Madam, being left in my hands by the author to introduce to the public, I thought myself obliged to say thus much in its defence, and that it was also a duty upon me to choose a patroness proper for it, and the author having pitched upon your name to do honour to some of her works, I thought your protection could be so useful to none as to this whose owning it may silence the malice of its enemies. Your wit and judgment being to be submitted to in all cases, besides your natural tenderness and compassion for the unfortunate gives you in a manner another title to it. The preference which is due to you upon so many accounts is therefore the reason of this present address, for at the worst, if this play should be so unfortunate as not to be thought worthy of your acceptance, yet it is certain, that it's worth any man's while to have the honour of subscribing himself,

Madam,

Your Most Obedient Humble Servant, G.J.

Facing Page: William Vincent, *The Indian Queen*, c. 1690. This mezzotint is widely believed to depict the English actor Anne Bracegirdle (c. 1671–1748), who performed in the role of Queen Semernia in the 1689 production of *The Widow Ranter*. It was fashionable among very elite Europeans during this period to have enslaved Africans as personal attendants; the two children holding the Queen's train and umbrella are likely intended to echo this fashion and thus signify to English viewers the Queen's high status.

---

1   *Newgate*   London's main prison.

from Nathaniel Bacon, *Manifesto Concerning the Present Troubles in Virginia* (1676)

Bacon's *Manifesto* comprises his own defense against the accusations of rebellion and treason leveled against him for his decision to take up arms against the Indigenous peoples with whom the Virginia government had treaties. Bacon expresses disgust with what he deems the ineffectual and self-interested policies of the colonial rulers who, in his opinion, lack the education, experience, and wisdom to protect the colony. Not only does this document present Bacon's view that he acted virtuously and in the best interest of the colonists, it also indicates that Bacon's violence against Indigenous groups was indiscriminate.

If virtue be a sin, if piety be guilt, all the principles of morality, goodness, and justice be perverted, we must confess that those who are now called rebels may be in danger of those high imputations, those loud and several bulls,[1] would affright innocents and render the defence of our brethren and the inquiry into our sad and heavy oppressions, treason. But if there be, as sure there is, a just God to appeal to, if religion and justice be a sanctuary here, if to plead the cause of the oppressed, if sincerely to aim at his Majesty's honour and the public good without any reservation or by interest, if to stand in the gap after so much blood of our dear brethren brought and sold, if after the loss of a great part of his Majesty's colony deserted and dispeopled, freely with our lives and estates to endeavor to save the remainders be treason, God almighty judge and let guilty die. But since we cannot in our hearts find one single spot of rebellion or treason or that we have in any manner aimed at subverting the settled government or attempting[2] of the person of any either magistrate or private man—notwithstanding the several reproaches and threats of some who for sinister ends were disaffected to us and censured our innocent and honest designs—and since all people in all places where we have yet been can attest our civil quiet peaceable behaviour far

---

1 *bulls* Official documents or edicts.
2 *attempting* Threatening or attacking.

different from that of rebellion and tumultuous persons, let truth be bold and all the world know the real foundations of pretended guilt, we appeal to the country itself what end of what nature their oppressions have been or by what cabal[1] and mystery the designs of many of those whom we call great men have been transacted and carried on. But let us trace these men in authority and favour to whose hand the dispensation of the country's wealth has been committed. Let us observe the sudden rise of their estates composed with the quality of which they first entered this country or the reputation they have held here amongst wise and discerning men, and let us see whether their extractions and education have not been vile, and by what pretense of learning and virtue they could so soon into employments of so great trust and consequence, let us consider their sudden advancement and let us also consider whether any public work for our safety and defense or for the advancement and propagation of trade, liberal arts or sciences is here extant in any [way] adequate to our vast charge. Now let us compare these things together and see what sponges have sucked up the public treasure and whether it hath not been privately contrived away by unworthy favourites and juggling parasites whose tottering fortunes have been repaired and supported at the public charge. Now if it be so judged what greater guilt can be than to offer to pry into these and to unriddle the mysterious wiles of a powerful cabal; let all people judge what can be of more dangerous import than to suspect the so long safe proceedings of some of our grandees and whether people may with safety open their eyes in so nice[2] a concern.

Another main article of our guilt is our open manifest aversion of all, not only the foreign but the protected and darling Indians,[3] this we are informed is rebellion of a deep dye for that both the Governor and Council are by Colonel Coale's[4] assertion bound to defend the

---

1   *cabal* Secretive political meeting.

2   *nice* Difficult.

3   *protected and darling Indians* I.e., those Indigenous groups who had formed alliances with the colonists.

4   *Colonel Coale* William Cole, a member of the governor's council in Virginia during and after Bacon's Rebellion; during the early parts of the rebellion he worked as a mediator between Bacon and the colonial government, but he eventually sided with Governor Berkeley.

Queen[1] and the Appomatocks[2] with their blood. Now whereas we do declare and can prove that they have been for these many years enemies to the king and country, robbers and thieves and invaders of his Majesty's right and our interest and estates, but yet have by persons in authority been defended and protected even against his Majesty's loyal subjects and that in so high a nature that even the complaints and oaths of his Majesty's most loyal subjects in a lawful manner proffered by them against those barbarous outlaws have been by the right honourable governor rejected and the delinquents from his presence dismissed not only with pardon and indemnity, but with all encouragement and favour, their firearms so destructfull to us and by our laws prohibited,[3] commanded to be restored to them, and open declaration before witness made that they must have ammunition although directly contrary to our law. Now what greater guilt can be than to oppose and endeavour the destruction of these honest quiet neighbours of ours.

Another main article of our guilt is our design not only to ruin and extirpate all Indians in general, but all manner of trade and commerce with them. Judge who can be innocent that strike at this tender eye of interest. Since the right honourable governor hath been pleased by his commission to warrant this trade, who dare oppose it, or opposing it can be innocent, although plantations be deserted, the blood of our dear brethren spilt, on all sides our complaints, continually murder upon murder renewed upon us. Who may or dare think of the general subversions of all manner of trade and commerce with our enemies; who can or dare impeach any of [the] traders at the heads of the rivers if, contrary to the wholesome provision made by laws for the country's safety, they dare continue their illegal practices and dare asperse the right honourable governor's wisdom and justice so highly to pretend to have his warrant to break that law

---

1   *Queen*   Likely a reference to Cockacoeske (c. 1640–c. 1686), leader or Warowansqua of the Pamunkey during the period of Bacon's Rebellion.

2   *Appomatocks*   Algonquian-speaking people who inhabited what is now Virginia and had in previous decades been affiliated with the Pamunkey under the Powhatan Confederacy.

3   *their firearms ... prohibited*   One of Bacon's complaints stems from the colonial government's practice of trading guns and ammunition with Native Americans in exchange for fur and other luxury goods. For ordinary citizens of the colony, the selling of weapons to Native Americans was strictly regulated, and had been forbidden outright at various points prior to the rebellion.

which himself made; who dare say that these men at the heads of the rivers buy and sell our blood, and do still, notwithstanding the late act made to the contrary, admit Indians painted and continue to commerce, although things can be proved yet who dare be so guilty as to do it.

from *Strange News from Virginia: Being a Full and True Account of the Life and Death of Nathaniel Bacon* (1677)

Pamphlets like this one were a popular way for people to learn of current events. *Strange News from Virginia* circulated in London in 1677 and contains information about Nathaniel Bacon's background, his initial altercations with the Susquehannock people, and the responses of the Virginian government. It is likely that Aphra Behn was aware of this publication and drew on it for her play. The pamphlet outlines the details of Bacon's rebellion and recounts his eventual death.

This Gentleman, who has of late beckoned the attention of all men of understanding who are any ways desirous of novelty, or care what becomes of any part of the world besides that themselves live in, had the honour to be descended of an ancient and honourable family. His name, Nathaniel Bacon, to which to the long-known title of Gentleman by his long study in the Inns of Court he has since added that of Esquire.[1] He was the son of Mr. Thomas Bacon, of an ancient seat known by the denomination of Freestone Hall in the County of Suffolk, a Gentleman of known loyalty and ability. His father as he was able so he was willing to allow this his son a very gentle competency[2] to subsist upon, but he as it proved having a soul too

---

1   *Inns of Court … Esquire*   Since the Middle Ages, London's Inns of Court had been a group of four institutions responsible for providing education in and oversight of the legal profession in England and Wales. The title of "Esquire," used in conjunction with a reference to the Inns of Court, is meant to imply that Bacon had some legal training.
2   *competency*   Inheritance or income.

large for that allowance could not contain himself within bounds;[1] which his careful father perceiving, and also that he had a mind to travel (having seen diverse parts of the world before) consented to his inclination of going to Virginia. ...

That plantation which he chose to settle in is generally known by the name of Curles,[2] situated in the upper part of the James River, and the time of his revolt was not till the beginning of March 1675/6.[3] At which time the Susquo-hannan[4] Indians (a known enemy to that country),[5] having made an insurrection and killed diverse of the English, amongst whom it was his fortune to have a servant slain; in revenge of whose death, and other damages he received from those turbulent Susquohanians, without the Governor's[6] consent he furiously took up arms against them, and was so fortunate as to put them to flight, but not content therewith; the aforesaid Governor hearing of his eager pursuit after the vanquished Indians, sent out a select company of soldiers to command him to desist; but he instead of listening thereunto, persisted in his revenge, and sent to the Governor to intreat his commission, that he might more cheerfully prosecute his design; which being denied him by the messenger he sent for that purpose, he notwithstanding continued to make head with his own servants, and other English then resident in Curles, against them.

---

1 *having ... bounds* A gentle way of suggesting that young Nathaniel spent more money than his inheritance would allow.

2 *Curles* Now known as Curles Neck, in Henrico County, Virginia.

3 *March 1675/6* Until 1752—when all of Great Britain joined the rest of Europe in adopting the Gregorian calendar—England, Wales, Ireland, and the American colonies used a different calendar than did Scotland, which resulted in some discrepancies in marking the change of the new year. The dual date indicates a situation where a discrepancy exists.

4 *Susquo-hannan* Reference to the Susquehannock, an Iroquoian-speaking people; their trade routes had for many years included coastal Virginia, but only recently had they begun to establish ongoing residence in that territory, as English colonial expansion and conflict with the Iroquois Confederacy had driven them further south.

5 *known enemy to that country* Reference to the recurrent conflicts between the Susquehannock and the more powerful Algonquian-speaking people, such as the Powhatan, who lived in the area.

6 *Governor* The acting Governor of Jamestown would have been Sir William Berkeley, who held office from 1660 to 1677.

from *More News from Virginia, being A True and Full Relation of all Occurrences in that Country, since the Death of Nathaniel Bacon* (1677)

A sequel to *Strange News*, this pamphlet provides additional information about the circumstances surrounding Nathaniel Bacon's rebellion. The existence of this second pamphlet indicates that the incident remained of ongoing interest in London. *More News* offers additional details about the revolt and its aftermath—specifically the executions of Bacon's officers—gleaned from a letter written by Admiral John Berry (1636–90), a royal commissioner who was sent to the colonies to restore order after the uprising.

In our last we gave you an account of part of the life and the last exit of Bacon, the grand opposer of the Royal Party in Virginia; but then our intelligence reached no farther than his death. We could not inform you of a certain peace, nor give you an account of the arrival of those soldiers which, by his Majesty's order, went under the command of the honourable Sir John Berry, Admiral to the four ships sent lately to Virginia, which now by a letter arrived no longer ago than yesterday, written by the honourable Sir Jon Berry's own hand to a friend in London, we are fully enabled to do. This letter was dated the third of February last; wherein, after some occasional discourse to his friend, he proceeded after this following manner.

When we put off from the Downs,[1] we were distressed with bad weather and contrary winds; insomuch that we were in great fear, lest we should have suffered for want of fresh water. But after a ten weeks' hardship at sea, through the mercy of God, we safely arrived at Virginia on the 29 of January last; where contrary to our expectations, we found that Mr. Bacon had been two months before dead,[2] and that the Royal Party

---

1   *the Downs* Area of safe anchorage off the coast of Kent, England.
2   *Mr. Bacon … dead* Bacon died suddenly on 26 October 1676, from a mixture of typhus and dysentery known as "bloody flux."

had reduced the remaining rebels to obedience; and had (as it is requisite in all illegal insurrections) secured in prison some of the most notorious offenders. (Amongst the which none was so remarkable as one Giles Bland;[1] of whom Sir John Berry gives us this character.) That since it hath been his fortune formerly to have had some acquaintance with his relations, he is somewhat troubled for their sakes that he cannot do him a kindness.

But his actions by report have been so incredibly evil, and his trial being referred to common law, he does more than doubt[2] it will go hard with him.

This is the sum of Sir John Berry's letter; but because he would oblige his friend, to whom he writ, he procured the abstract of the names and characters of those persons who have been lately executed for their rebellion against the Royal Party in Virginia: so the enclosed paper is entitled, and these are the contents of it, as near as I could copy it, expressing its sense.

First one Johnson, who was a stirrer up of the people, but no fighter, deservedly died.

The next that was executed was one Farlow[3] (a chip off the old block of the rebellion), one of Cromwell's soldiers,[4] and taken with forty men coming to surprise me at Accomack.

The third was one Carver,[5] a valiant stout seaman, and taken miraculously, being all too besmeared with blood, and as we after learnt, came to surprise me at my quarters.

The fourth was one Wilford,[6] an interpreter, who frightened

---

1 *Giles Bland*   English colonist (c. 1647–77) who worked as a customs collector in Virginia until a series of conflicts with the authorities led to his dismissal in 1675. He was arrested for his participation in Bacon's Rebellion and executed in March 1677.

2 *doubt*   Suspect.

3 *Farlow*   George Farlow (1631–76).

4 *Cromwell's soldiers*   I.e., the soldiers fighting under the Parliamentarian Oliver Cromwell during the English Civil War, which resulted in the execution of Charles I and the inauguration of the Commonwealth, ruled by Oliver Cromwell from 1653 to 1658. The Commonwealth officially ended in 1660 with the restoration of Charles II.

5 *Carver*   William Carver (d. 1676).

6 *Wilford*   Thomas Wilford (1618–76).

by the Queen of Pomonkes[1] from the land she had granted her assembly a month after the peace was concluded with her.

The fifth who was executed, was one *Hansford*,[2] a valiant, stout and most resolved rebel, who would not be daunted at peril, nor persuaded by any civility, but made it his business after many overtures of kindness offered him, to act rebelliously himself, and infect the people.[3]

from *A True Narrative of the Late Rebellion in Virginia by the Royal Commissioners* (1676)

This document, prepared for King Charles II, details the events that led to Bacon's Rebellion. Although it can't be verified, it seems that Behn must have drawn from this document for some of her plot points. This report is the most thoroughly researched and least sensationalized recounting of the events that led to the rebellion, including Bacon's interactions with Pamunkey leader Cockacoeske (c. 1640–c. 1686), known to the English as "the Queen of the Pamunkey." Additionally, this text describes Bacon's tactic of kidnapping the wives and female relatives of the Virginian council to use as collateral. Interestingly, Behn's play romanticizes Bacon's interactions with the characters she calls the "Indian King and Queen," and though she includes the abduction of the women, she treats the event as comical; the women seem to respond to it as a madcap adventure, not as a dangerous war tactic.

Bacon having got about three hundred men together in arms prepared to go out against the Indians, the Governor and his friends endeavour to divert his designs, but cannot.

---

1   *Queen of Pomonkes*   Refers to Cockacoeske (c. 1640–c. 1686), leader or Warowansqua of the Pamunkey, an Algonquian-speaking people of what became Virginia. Cockacoeske represented a coalition of tribes which negotiated a peace with the colonists in 1677.

2   *Hansford*   Thomas Hansford (c. 1646–76).

3   Here ends the first part of Berry's list of people executed following Bacon's Rebellion; the list goes on to name eight more people executed at later dates, and Berry claims that at least five more unnamed participants may have been executed.

He proclaims Bacon and his followers rebels and mutineers for going forth against the Indians without a commission, and (getting a company of gentlemen together) the Governor marcheth up to the falls of James River[1] to pursue and take Bacon, or to seize him at his return; but all in vain, for Bacon had got over the river with his forces and hastening away into the woods, went directly and fell upon the Indians and killed some of them who were our best friends of Indians and had fought against the Susquahanocks enemies to the English.[2]

The Governor having issued forth a proclamation imposing no commerce with the reputed Indian enemies, besides the clogs[3] and conditions which were put on the garrisons placed or to be placed in the new erected forts, enjoining them not to make any attempt upon the Indians until they should first give the Governor an account thereof, and receive orders from him therein, put many to a stand, made the people expostulate and say how shall we know our enemies from our friends, are not the Indians all of a colour, and if we must not defend ourselves before they oppose us, they may take their usual advantage of surprise, and so destroy us ere we are capable of making any resistance. So that after all that charge in erecting of forts, after all the troubles of the congress of our forces, after all their toil and diligence used in discovering the enemy (who are seldom to be dealt with but in their own way of surprise) the very point of execution was to be determined of by a person residing in all likelihood at least a hundred miles distant from the place of action, to the loss of opportunities and utter discouragement of the soldiers and ourselves. Besides of what security were these forts to be, when the Indians cut off and destroyed diverse people within a small distance of the forts and some of the very soldiers in them, and they not daring to stir out to relieve any that were in danger and distress, themselves being

---

1   *the falls of James River*   The location of one of Bacon's properties in Virginia, which became known as "Bacon's Quarter."

2   *Susquahanocks ... English*   Relations between European colonists and the various Indigenous peoples established in the region were delicate and complex and doubtless exacerbated pre-existing rivalries between Indigenous nations in the region. The Algonquian-speaking Pamunkey had been among the first to enter into trade agreements with the colonizers; the Iroquoian-speaking Susquehannock fought against both the English and the Pamunkey during Bacon's Rebellion.

3   *clogs*   Impediments or obstructions.

scarce secure upon the place they were posted on. Nor would the people understand any distinction of friendly Indians and Indian enemies, for at that time it was impossible to distinguish one nation from another, they being deformed with paint of many colors, and at best (say they) who is he that can do it, for there was never any open or free trade among us that we might know them, but the whole trade monopolized by the Governor and Grandees.[1] ...

The bad weather abating he [Bacon] proceeds on his march and in a short time falls into a path of the Indians which lead to a main one which made him imagine himself to be near their main camp; but by the scouts sent out for discovery, he found nothing more yet than a continued large path and woods, which made them break the order of marching, and for expedition and conveniency to march at random, so continuing all along till this path brought them to a point, on each side whereof and before it was a swamp; upon which point the Pamunkey Indians had several cabins.

Some Indian scouts were sent out before the discovery (which were about ten Indians for the service of Bacon's army) who being espied by the contrary party of Indians they let them come up so nigh as to fire at them, which gave alarm to the English, who riding down in great disorder and haste to the Point (being about half a mile distance off) the Indians broke to the very edge of the swamp, which proved so mirey that Bacon and his men were presently at a ne plus ultra,[2] so that the mighty deal that was done at this time was only the taking of a little Indian child, and the killing of an Indian woman.

It chanced that the Queen of Pamunkey[3] with several of her principal Indians and others was not far off when this onset happened and had notice of Bacon's approach on her track of which her own scouts had made discovery to her, who leaving behind her all her goods and Indian corn,[4] vessels etc., and as much as she could to

---

1   *Grandees*   High-ranking persons.
2   *mirey*   Swampy or muddy;   *ne plus ultra*   Impasse.
3   *Queen of Pamunkey*   Cockacoeske (c. 1640–c. 1686), leader or Warowansqua of the Pamunkey nation. At this time, the Pamunkey had a delicate alliance with the Virginia government. It is likely that Behn modeled Semernia, the "Indian Queen" in *The Widow Ranter*, after her.
4   *Indian corn*   I.e., maize.

decline all occasion of offending the English whom she ever so much loved and reverenced, privately obscured from them, charging her own Indians that if they found the English coming upon them that they should neither fire a gun nor draw an arrow upon them.

It so happened in the stifling pursuit that they light[1] on an old Indian woman that was the Queen's nurse, whom they took prisoner and hoped she would be their guide to find out those Indians that had fled. But instead of directing them that way she led them quite contrary. So that following her for the remainder of that and almost another day, perceiving themselves misled by her and little likelihood of meeting with them, Bacon gave the command to his soldiers to knock her in the head, which they did, and they left her dead on the way.

from *The Beginning, Progress and Conclusion of Bacon's Rebellion in Virginia, in the years 1675 & 1676*, reprinted in Peter Force, *Tracts and other papers, relating principally to the origin, settlement, and progress of the Colonies in North America, from the discovery of the country to the year 1776* (1886)

These excerpts comprise an anonymous eyewitness account of Pamunkey leader Cockacoeske visiting the Council of Jamestown in June of 1676; the nineteenth-century historian Peter Force claims that the account had been "written thirty years after [Bacon's Rebellion] took place, by a person intimately acquainted with its origin, progress, and conclusion." Cockacoeske was a powerful political leader who negotiated treaties with the colonists after the end of Bacon's Rebellion. Behn seems to have used a description of her in the Commissioner's Report compiled for King Charles II (see the excerpts from *A True Narrative of the Late Rebellion in Virginia*, above)

---

1   *light* Alighted.

as a model for the character of Queen Semernia in *The Widow Ranter*. Cockacoeske appeared before the council to respond to their request that she provide men to assist the Virginian government in their struggles against hostile Indigenous nations.

Our committee being sat, the Queen of Pamunkey (descended from Oppechankenough[1] a former Emperor of Virginia) was introduced, who entered the chamber with a comportment graceful to admiration, bringing on her right hand an Englishman interpreter, and on the left her son a stripling twenty years of age, she having round her head a plait of black and white wampum peague[2] three inches broad in imitation of a crown, and was clothed in a mantle of dressed deer skins with the hair outwards and the edge cut round 6 inches deep which made strings resembling twisted fringe from the shoulders to the feet; thus with grave, courtlike gestures and a majestic air in her face, she walked up our long room to the lower end of the table, where after a few entreaties she sat down. The interpreter and her son standing by her on either side as they had walked up, our chairman asked her what men she would lend us for guides in the wilderness and to assist us against our enemy Indians; she spake to the interpreter to inform her what the chairman said (though we believed she understood him), he told us she bid him ask her son to whom the English tongue was familiar, and who was reputed the son of an English colonel, yet neither would he speak to or seem to understand the chairman but the interpreter told us, he referred all to his mother, who being again urged she after a little musing with an earnest passionate countenance as if tears were ready to gush out and a fervent sort of expression made a harangue about a quarter of an hour, often interlacing (with a high shrill voice and vehement passion) these words "Tatapatamoi[3] Chepiack" (i.e., Tatapatamoi dead).

---

1   *Oppechankenough*   Opechancanough was Paramount Chief of the Powhatan Confederacy, a powerful alliance of numerous Algonquian-speaking nations residing in what is now Virginia, from 1618 until his death in 1646. Opechancanough is generally believed to have been Cockacoeske's father.

2   *wampum peague*   Small, cylindrical beads used by many Indigenous peoples for various purposes including trade, record-keeping, and adornment, often strung together and woven into belts.

3   *Tatapatamoi*   Husband of Cockacoeske, who had served as *werowance* of the Pamunkey until his death in 1656, after which Cockacoeske took up leadership.

Col. Hill,[1] being next me, shook his head, I asked him what was the matter, he told me all she said was too true to our shame, and that his father was general in that battle, where diverse years before Tatapatamoi her husband had led a hundred of his Indians in help to the English against our former enemy Indians, and was there slain with most of his men; for which no compensation (at all) had been to that day rendered to her wherewith she now upbraided us.

Her discourse ending and our morose chairman not advancing one cold word towards assuaging the anger and grief her speech and demeanour manifested under her oppression, nor taking any notice of all she had said, neither considering that we (then) were in our great exigency, supplicants to her for a favour of the same kind as the former, for which we did not deny the having been so ingrate, he rudely pushed again the same question, "what Indians will you now contribute, etc.?" Of this disregard she signified her resentment by a disdainful aspect, and turning her head half aside, sat mute till that same question being pressed a third time, she not returning her face to the board, answered with a low slighting voice in her own language, "six," but being further importuned she sitting a little while sullen, without uttering a word between said "twelve," though she then had a hundred and fifty Indian men, in her town, and so rose up and gravely walked away as not pleased with her treatment.

Facing Page: This map of Virginia and the Chesapeake region created by English colonist John Smith was first published in 1612, but it remained the primary map used by colonists until the 1670s. In the upper lefthand corner is an illustration depicting the powerful Powhatan chief Wahunsonacock (c. 1547–c. 1618; generally referred to by the English as simply "Powhatan"); he was an ancestor of the Pamunkey leader Cockacoeske. The Powhatan/ James River, site of both Jamestown and, further upriver, Nathaniel Bacon's plantation, appears just beneath and to the right of this illustration.

---

1   *Col. Hill*   Likely reference to Colonel Edward Hill (1637–1700), who fought to put down Bacon's Rebellion.

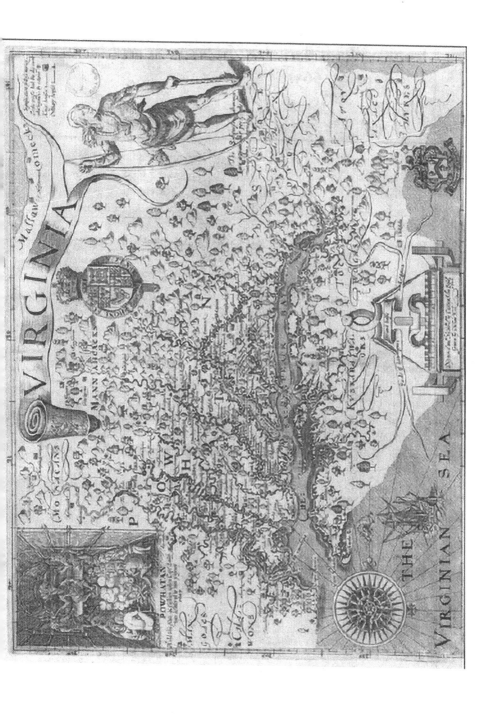

from William Berkeley, *A Discourse and View of Virginia* (1663)

William Berkeley served his second term as governor of the colony of Virginia from 1660 to 1677, a period that included Bacon's Rebellion. In this text, Berkeley describes the various natural resources present in the Virginian colony and surrounding areas, and he discusses the difficulties experienced by the early "planters," or colonists, as they tried to establish themselves and send merchandise back to England.

Before I enter into the consideration of the advantages this kingdom of England has by the plantation[1] in Virginia, I think it necessary to make a short description of the situation of it, as to the climate; and then tell what natural helps it has to make it a glorious and flourishing country. And when this discourse shall produce a concession of the natural advantages it has above all other His Majesty's Plantations, I shall lay down the causes, both intrinsic and accidental, why it has not in all this supposed long tract of time produced those rich and staple commodities, which I shall in this discourse affirm it is capable of.

And, first, for the climate: It lieth within the degrees of 37 and 42. (Maryland included.) Which by all is confessed to be a situation capable of the diversities of all northern and southern commodities, some drugs and spices excepted, which Florida,[2] on whose borders we are newly seated, may also probably produce.

Into the Bay of Virginia, formerly called Chesapeack Bay, run six eminent rivers, none twenty miles distant from another; three of which exceed the Thames,[3] both in extent and progression of the tides; these cause and continue the admired fertility of the country, and by their greatness and contiguity temper those heats which the dryer places of Africa are subject to, in the same degrees of latitude.

Up these rivers ships of three hundred tons sail near two hundred

---

1 *plantation* I.e., colony.
2 *Florida* In 1663, when this piece was written, Florida was occupied by Spanish colonies and comprised a much larger region than it does today. It remained a colony of Spain until after the Seven Years' War in 1763.
3 *the Thames* Major river in London.

miles, and anchor in the fresh waters; and by this means are not troubled with those worms which endamage ships, both in the Western Islands of America,[1] and in the Mediterranean Sea. And to avoid a larger discourse of it, I will here note it, that our ships, once past the land's end, are in no danger of pirates, rocks, or lee shores, till they come to their port, and fewer ships miscarry going to Virginia, than to any port at that distance in the world.[2]

Now for those things which are naturally in it, they are these: iron, lead, pitch, tar, masts, timber for ships of the greatest magnitude, and wood for pot-ashes.

Those other commodities, which are produced by industry, are flax, hemp, silk, wheat, barley, oats, rice, cotton, all sorts of pulse and fruits, the last of which in that perfection, that if the taste were the only judge, we would not think they were of the same species with those from which they are derived to us from England. The vicious ruinous plant of tobacco[3] I would not name, but that it brings more money to the Crown than all the islands in America besides.

Now this is ascertained and confessed, that such staple commodities as iron, silk, flax, hemp, and pot-ashes may be easily raised in Virginia, an high imputation will lie upon us, why we have not all this time endeavoured to evidence the truth and certainty of it, to our own and the public advantage.

To this I will answer, that the long time of seating of Virginia is a general and popular error: for though the first ships arrived in Virginia in 1606, yet by reason of many almost insuperable difficulties, the increase of the number of planters was hardly perceptible. For first, that,[4] as all uncleared plantations, was unwholesome; then all they eat came from England,[5] and provided for those they never

---

1   *Western Islands of America*   Meaning the Caribbean.

2   *Up these rivers … world*   It was common for ships to sail into the Chesapeake Bay and up the rivers to bring them closer to the settlements. As Berkeley observes, this practice kept the ships safe from the dangers they would face if anchored in the Atlantic Ocean.

3   *vicious ruinous plant of tobacco*   Berkeley shares the disdain of many contemporaries who had come to see the smoking of tobacco—which had quickly grown popular, if not indispensable, throughout Europe—as a "vice."

4   *that*   I.e., Virginia.

5   *For first … from England*   Initial attempts at planting crops in Virginia were unsuccessful for a variety of reasons, and the colonists subsisted almost entirely on food brought from England.

saw nor cared for, was not likely to be very good. Then the Indians quickly grew jealous of them, and forced them to fight for every foot of ground they held, and in the year 1622, in one night murdered all but four or five hundred.[1] So that from that time we must begin the account of the plantation. Nor is this all, for many years after this, the danger and scarcity of the inhabitants was so famed through England, that none but such as were forced could be induced to plant[2] or defend the place; and of those that came, there was not one woman to thirty men, and *populus virorum*[3] is of no long duration anywhere. But since the year 1630, the place began to be of more plenty and security, for the Indians, though not subdued, were terrified to a suspension of arms, the planters then first began to fence their grounds and plant corn; the few cattle they had, increased to such numbers that they were able to help their neighbour plantations. And now I believe that there is no plantation of the English would more abound in cattle, hogs, and all sorts of fruit, than Virginia, if they had but a mean price to quicken their industry and make their providence vigilant.

Facing Page: This woodcut appeared on the title page of a pamphlet titled *The Ranters Ranting*, published in London in 1650. The short work purports to expose the scandalous behaviors of a group of Ranters who had been arrested earlier that year, which allegedly included mixed-gender gatherings in which attendants sang blasphemous songs and engaged in drunken and sexually charged dancing. Sensational, condemnatory documents such as this one are among the only extant contemporary sources for information about the Ranters. (Call number R450, image 16735, used by permission of the Folger Shakespeare Library.)

---

1   *in the year ... hundred*   This event is known as the Jamestown Massacre or the Powhatan Uprising. On 22 March 1622, the Powhatan retaliated against the English colonists in Virginia who had been gradually encroaching on their land for tobacco plantations. Three hundred and forty-seven colonists died in the attack, which almost wiped out the colony.
2   *plant*   I.e., colonize.
3   *populous virorum*   Latin: population of men.

The Ranters Ranting :

With

The apprehending, examinations, and confession of *Iohn Collins*, *I. Shakespear*, *Tho. Wiberton*, and five more which are to answer the next Sessions. And severall songs or catches, which were sung at their meetings. Also their severall kinds of mirth, and dancing. Their blasphemous opinions. Their belief concerning heaven and hell. And the reason why one of the same opinion cut off the heads of his own mother and brother. Set forth for the further discovery of this ungodly crew.

LONDON

Printed by *B. Alsop*, 1650.

From the Publisher

A name never says it all, but the word "Broadview" expresses a good deal of the philosophy behind our company. We are open to a broad range of academic approaches and political viewpoints. We pay attention to the broad impact book publishing and book printing has in the wider world; for some years now we have used 100% recycled paper for most titles. Our publishing program is internationally oriented and broad-ranging. Our individual titles often appeal to a broad readership too; many are of interest as much to general readers as to academics and students.

Founded in 1985, Broadview remains a fully independent company owned by its shareholders—not an imprint or subsidiary of a larger multinational.

To order our books or obtain up-to-date information, please visit broadviewpress.com.

broadview press
www.broadviewpress.com

This book is made of paper from well-managed FSC® - certified forests, recycled materials, and other controlled sources.